Dismantling Diversity M

Global diversity and inclusion management practice is in a state of arrested development. Leaders and practitioners are caught in grooves that are no longer effective, if they ever were. In *Dismantling Diversity Management*, Dr. Jude Smith Rachele takes a big leap in propounding that businesses, given the incredible complexity of the world's social, economic, and political fabric, must embrace morality and not just seek to act merely for reasons of legal compliance or profit. It presents a joined-up system of diversity, which also extends beyond human resources into the wider fields of organization and leadership development.

The book emphasizes the vital importance of ethical and values-driven leadership and of living, not just spouting out, corporate values. Jude provides a valuable contribution to the international field of diversity management as she highlights the key flaws in traditional diversity management thinking, and presents to the reader a clear picture of the barriers in place that make it difficult for practitioners, leaders, and all of those committed to social justice to achieve desired outcomes within organizations. This book is a courageous and refreshing look at diversity. It not only provides a bold critique of how corporate structure has co-opted people into a diversity management model that perpetuates, rather than transforms the status quo, it also maps out how to break this ineffective cycle.

Dismantling Diversity Management will be of interest to organizational development professionals, diversity and inclusion practitioners, senior executive officers, and human resource and talent management professionals.

Jude Smith Rachele, originally from the United States of America, has lived and worked internationally, across EMEA and the Americas. Having started her career as a diversity and inclusion specialist, she has branched out her practice to include business ethics, leadership, and organizational development. Jude holds a BA in Psychology, and a PhD in Business.

Dismantling Diversity Management

Introducing an Ethical Performance Improvement Campaign

Jude Smith Rachele

Routledge
Taylor & Francis Group

LONDON AND NEW YORK

First published 2017 by Routledge

2 Park Square, Milton Park, Abingdon, Oxfordshire OX14 4RN
52 Vanderbilt Avenue, New York, NY 10017

Routledge is an imprint of the Taylor & Francis Group, an informa business

First issued in paperback 2019

British Library Cataloguing-in-Publication Data
A catalogue record for this book is available from the British Library

Library of Congress Cataloging-in-Publication Data
A catalog record for this book has been requested

ISBN: 978-1-4724-5640-3 (hbk)
ISBN: 978-0-367-88067-5 (pbk)

Typeset in Bembo
by codeMantra

Contents

Figure

Foreword

Diversity can often seem a dry topic, involving audits and box-ticking, and pressure to comply with political correctness. Just counting things can seem to be a way of avoiding the underlying issues which concern people.

Diversity management should be about unleashing creativity and engagement from across the workforce, recognizing that innovation derives from people.

Jude Smith Rachele enters this field as a breath of fresh air, bringing energy and enthusiasm which can blow the dust off tired people and institutions. She draws on a wealth of practical experience from both sides of the Atlantic, and from public and private sectors.

Unusually, as a consultant, Jude subjected herself to the demands of a university PhD. She maintained her practical focus, and took on an ambitious extended Action Research project at a large further education college. Having completed her thesis, she recognized the value of adapting it into a book to reach a wider audience.

The book should not simply be seen as the culmination of many years of research at Exeter and Kingston Universities, but as a starting point for a fresh view of organizational change. The "Diversity Quality Cycle", which Jude devised and piloted, demonstrates how change at the level of strategic management can be brought about, or frustrated.

Strategy need not simply be equated with finance. The stakes are high. We cannot afford to continue to waste the organization's key resource: the people.

Richard Ennals
Emeritus Professor, Corporate Responsibility and Working Life,
Kingston University, United Kingdom
Professor, Working Life and Innovation, University of Agder, Norway
Professor, Skill and Technology, Linnaeus University, Sweden

Preface

I love diversity and the richness that it brings. I do not always agree, or feel comfortable or safe with all of the diversity of opinions and perspectives that I see and hear. However, as a person who seeks and embraces growth and development, and who is happy to venture into unknown cultures and territories to learn new things about others and myself, I live and value diversity, and above all else, justice. This modus operandi has given me life experiences that have taken me to great heights, and to rock bottoms. But, no matter where it has taken, or continues to take me, I am convinced, whole-heartedly and intellectually, that exposure to differences, to variations on our own mundane, and sometimes fearful and ignorant beliefs and thoughts yields tremendous insight, strength, courage, integrity, and creativity.

I am compelled to write this book because of my deep concern about what I can only call "diversity inertia" within the field of diversity management. It happens when strategic plans either fail to be implemented, or fail in their execution. I have experienced it over and over again. It appears to be preventing many diversity management initiatives from yielding tangible and/or sustainable improvements of social justice outcomes, not just for minority groups, but for all people. Something is not bending. It is this inflexibility, this resistance, that I have sought to understand in order to enable true transformation, rather than superficial organizational or societal change. We need to go deeper if we are going to break the stasis of diversity management as it stands today.

In 1993, at the very beginning of my career, I was introduced to the concept of diversity management. I entered into, and have remained true to, this field ever since. Diversity management, for me, can be defined as:

> A process intended to create and maintain a positive environment where the similarities and differences of individuals are valued, so that all can reach their potential and maximize their contributions to an organization's strategic goals and objectives.[1]

In the early days, I recall my father's reaction to my newly found profession. He was a trailblazer for social justice and racial equality, and I thought he would be proud of my chosen path. To my complete dismay, he was not pleased. As a matter of fact, he was incensed.

He declared, as an African-American male born in the 1920s, "*I've* been managing diversity my whole damn life!" For him it was never an option not to do so; his success, and, even at times, his life had depended upon it. That diversity management had become a modern day corporate initiative offended him deeply. He never believed in it, and was always deeply suspicious of it. Now having worked in this quasi-professional area for 22 years, I understand his point of view better.

In the past 40 years, we have made great strides in equality in the West. Legislation has been passed to help minorities gain the right to vote. We have legally desegregated societies. We have created better educational opportunities for underprivileged groups. We have made public transport more accessible for people with certain mobility needs. We have legalized same-sex marriages. These are all big wins and represent significant changes in our systems of legislature.

A lot has changed and improved; there is no denying progress. But we also should address directly the rising tides of resistance and disapproval, and the heightened sense of battle among and between opposing forces. In the light of all of our progress, it feels that we are faced with an unprecedented level of global diversity conflict. How much has actually stayed the same? How much has worsened? *Dismantling Diversity Management: Introducing an Ethical Performance Improvement Campaign* takes a critical look at diversity management practice and performance, and offers solutions that will help us to improve not only our practices, but the social justice outcomes these practices are designed to achieve for businesses and societies.

As a practitioner, I have delivered innumerous diversity training sessions to clients from a wide range of sectors, businesses, and countries. I enjoy teaching and raising people's levels of awareness and skills. I am, however, saddened to see how sparse and temporal improvements in social justice outcomes are on institutional and societal levels. What began decades ago has been instrumental in effecting some improvements in social and economic justice for traditional minority groups. Too much diversity management is been driven by superficial short-term vision, quick wins, legal compliance aimed at placating regulators and disgruntled employees. In the face of all this, not enough positive change has taken place, and I argue that with the current form of diversity management at the helms, organizations and societies have gone backward when it comes to improving social justice outcomes.

Some say it just takes time. Yes, it does. But time is not a silver bullet that can heal all wounds without us taking a proactive and courageous approach to changing outcomes. Minorities who have invested heavily in their own personal and career development may feel, as citizens of aging societies, that time is running out. Time is not a luxury they can afford if they are to get a return on their investment in their lifetime. This book explores who has created our current diversity management frameworks. Are things missing from its architecture? If so what might these be?

In my work, and in my travels, I have discovered that I am not alone in being bored by, dissatisfied with, and suspicious of diversity management. Many diversity practitioners and champions have confided their frustrations to me about how much they are struggling with diversity management, and how they feel stuck in a rut of rhetoric. It is time to find a way forward to put things on a better course for those who value and believe in the concept of social justice and diversity, so they are in a better position to achieve it.

The reality is, I do not abide by diversity management practices that I see as myopic, exclusive, discriminatory or unfair to a majority of people, even if it is for the relative advantage of traditionally underrepresented groups. My concerns are less with how many disabled people, or Black people (or People of Color), or women we have working in organizations, and more with creating more ethical leadership and fairer systems of governance. This is why *Dismantling Diversity Management: Introducing an Ethical Performance Improvement Campaign Journey* may be my diversity swan song.

I have found diversity management strategies neither liberating nor invigorating. What escapes scrutiny are the weaknesses within leadership and organizational cultures that prevent values from being realized. By delving into these institutional barriers to equality, diversity, and inclusion, *Dismantling Diversity Management: Introducing an Ethical Performance Improvement Campaign Journey* highlights elements of organizational status quos that prevent diversity management from being effective.

The challenge is to explore what is missing in the current dialogs and constructs that we have around diversity management. *Dismantling Diversity Management: Introducing an Ethical Performance Improvement Campaign Journey* takes a close, hard look at diversity management and whether or not, as it stands, it is an effective method for achieving greater social justice, creativity, profitability, or health and wellbeing for individuals, businesses, and societies. There is a tradition here that needs to be scrutinized and unpicked. We cannot assume that just because we have apparently well-intentioned legal and management systems, with apparently well-intentioned individuals running them, that these systems will achieve their goals, or that they will change present and future outcomes by creating and enabling people to benefit from new opportunities and new, and more equitable social outcomes.

One of the objectives of diversity management is to eradicate discrimination and prejudice within organizations, and individual belief systems, that unfairly disadvantage people. Diversity management is born out of decades of social activism.

Social activism is defined as:

> The promotion and guidance used to cultivate changes in business practices, business policies or the government to influence social change. The duties of a social activist include communicating with policy makers, researching for the cause, and organizing responses for the media.[2]

In exploring more fully the effectiveness of such practices, there appears to me to be a key conundrum that we have to address. Is it possible for diversity practitioners, and indeed other groups of key stakeholders, within the context of their organizational cultures, to act in accordance with the social activism that is the very spark of external societal and cultural transformation?

If diversity management is designed to ensure greater social justice within organizations, it is not currently working well enough, or fast enough. Many of the diversity management initiatives I have experienced over the decades have: been driven by human resources departments; been based upon short-term objectives, heavily focused upon increasing the demographic representation of certain social minority groups (i.e. women, people of color, people with disabilities, etc.); relied heavily upon diversity training to be a key organizational cultural game-changer; and been effective at achieving what are referred to within this book as micro-emancipations, yet have simultaneously, to a large extent, maintained organizational status quos. It is time for its dismantling and its reconstruction. If we do not do this now, we run the risk of another 40 years of mediocre, at best, diversity management practices.

This book dismantles diversity management from its foundation of human resources management, and reconstructs it upon the foundation of engaged, ethical, and enlightened leadership. Importantly, this book explores the relationship between effective diversity management, senior executive leadership, and governance. It explores the need for a more ethical, less superficial, and a more strategic long-term approach to diversity management. *Dismantling Diversity Management* moves away from the assumption. Fully appreciating this several years ago, I coined the phrase the Ethical Performance Improvement Campaign and have used this as the key transformative methodologies in enabling organizations to improve their diversity management practices.

I argue that the objective of diversity management should be to improve social justice outcomes both within organizations and wider society. I argue that what has been profoundly overlooked in a majority of diversity management are long-term strategies that take into account and that seek to improve the ethical climate of an organization. Getting diversity management right, and improving social justice outcomes is indeed an epic task, hence my introduction of the notion of an Ethical Performance Improvement Campaign (EPIC) Journey, which I believe should be at the forefront of strategic thinking and actions if diversity management is going to be more effective.

As a result of the years I have spent conducting academic research, and working as a diversity and inclusion practitioner within industry, I came to believe that diversity management initiatives were more likely to be successful in organizations that had strong ethical leadership that had a long-term vision and commitment to improving social outcomes. On the basis of that, I conceptualized a model of organizational transformation designed to enable diversity management to be more effective. This I call, and introduce within this book, the Ethical Performance Improvement Campaign (EPIC).

As part of this EPIC Journey, *Dismantling Diversity Management* also introduces a model of participative governance, the Diversity Quality Cycle, led by senior executives team, with a high level of employee engagement from across any given organization.

My work, to date, has enabled me to touch the lives of many for the good. Interestingly enough, the transformations that have been made are transformations that have been achieved mostly, but not exclusively, on personal levels. Empowering individuals is a worthwhile task. It helps people develop a greater awareness of themselves, taps clearly into their personal values and ethics, creates lives that support them, and helps them to mold the world around them rather than molding themselves around the world.

This book is written for those who care about, and who wish to disrupt the status quo of diversity management, and who want to change their world. It is written for individuals and/or groups who have responsibility for equality, diversity, and inclusion within their work or client organizations. It is also written for those who wield the power to effect social change. If we are lucky, these people are one and the same.

If we are not, then it is my hope that this book will give those who care greater voice, agency, and power within their organizations, and increase their capacity to effect change. These people include human resources professionals, equality, diversity and inclusion leads, business managers, members of employee resource groups, members of governing committees, and external diversity management consultants.

Aside from these professionals, this book is also for the many students who, over the years, have asked me to point them in the direction of textbooks on diversity management.

I write this book for sanity, my own and that of other leaders and diversity and inclusion practitioners who are frustrated by diversity management's direction of travel. We have gotten some things right, but I believe that weak organizational ethics contribute tremendously to failed and inadequate attempts of valuing and enhancing diversity within organizations. I also write this book for that critical mass of millennials out there who put purpose ahead of profit. What a disappointing world we must be showing you. We have done some good, but it falls to you to do better. Bon chance!

Jude Smith Rachele, PhD
Vermont, United States of America
November 8, 2016

Notes

1 Source: U.S. Department of Veterans' Affairs, Office of Diversity and Inclusion. (n.d.). Diversity Management. In *Glossary*. Retrieved May 8, 2009, from www.diversity.hr.va.gov/glossary.htm.
2 Retrieved August 20, 2015, from www.reference.com/world-view/social-activism-f976daed19cdd577.

1 Dismantling diversity management

To me, it really seems visible today that ethics is not something exterior to the economy, which, as technical matter, could function on its own; rather, ethics is an interior principle of the economy itself, which cannot function if it does not take account of the human values of solidarity and reciprocal responsibility.

—Pope Benedict XVI

If the future is to resemble the past less, if diversity inertia is to be overcome, and if better social justice outcomes are to be achieved, then we need to lay a stronger foundation upon which our diversity management strategies can be created and built. In order to do so, institutional transformations have to take place. This requires courage from senior executives and leaders. The time to develop this courage is now. Now is the time to dismantle traditional diversity management frameworks, to make informed judgments about which elements are best left in the past and which are best to carry into the future, and to determine what novel approaches are required to meet the demands of the twenty-first-century business environment.

We may be doing ourselves, and others, an enormous disservice, to say nothing of wasting an inordinate amount of time and resources, if we ignore the detrimental impacts that unhealthy, unethical organizations can have on an individual's sense of self-worth, hope for the future, and belief in business leadership. While the journey to social justice is epic, and often frustrating for people still working toward social justice, we can be using our time more wisely. This chapter outlines several reasons examining why it is time to dismantle traditional diversity management frameworks.

Short-termism and shareholder primacy

Diversity management theories and practices are positioned within the wider model of the business economy. Traditionally, behavior in this economy has been fueled by short-term profit maximization. This mentality is very much represented in current diversity management thinking and discourse. Organizations are looking for economic "quick wins" and "silver bullets."

In his article, "The fatal flaws of diversity and the business case for ethnic minorities," Mike Noon (2007) states:

> Employers take a short-term focus for business reasons; not least the requirement in the private sector to satisfy the needs of financiers and shareholders … If the benefits of equal opportunity initiatives are only realizable five to ten years in the future,

they are considerably less persuasive for managers required to produce short-term benefits for their shareholders and who might themselves have performance bonuses based on short-term targets.

The setting of short-term numerical targets to improve demographic representation of underrepresented groups is widespread. However, it is an approach that is unsustainable, unenlightened, and unhelpful.

Diversity management strategies are most effective when they are based upon strong data linked to business performance. Within the tradition of diversity management, there is an established practice of collecting demographic data related to legally protected characteristics. These characteristics include race, gender, disability, age, sexual orientation, marital status/civil partnership, pregnancy/maternity, and gender identity. It is considered best practice for organizations to capture this data. Nonetheless, because there is often a lack of clarity and leadership around the diversity management agenda, many organizations express insecurity when it comes to collecting such data. This data, however, is what makes it possible for diversity and inclusion researchers to conduct their work, and to draw conclusions about organizational effectiveness.

Frequently, diversity management initiatives are focused upon improving organizational demographics. For instance, it is often said that organizations need more women on Boards, or that we need more women in the tech industry. Clearly, measurements need to be in place in order to demonstrate whether or not diversity objectives are met. If thorough disciplined data collection is not achieved, diversity management is relegated to a quasi-scientific profession. Strong data is required in order to prove points. If practitioners are prevented from collecting this data, then it makes it impossible for them to legitimize their practice.

Demographic data alone, however, is not the only, or best, measure of effective diversity management. We also need data that explores the ethical climates that can be analyzed in relation to demographic data. Organizations may do well achieving short-term wins, and increasing the number of people from underrepresented groups, but the organizational cultures within which these people have to work may still be riddled with prejudice, poor decision-making, corporate corruption, and a variety of other ethical issues.

Achieving greater social justice for all people, through diversity management, is no quick fix. Many of us who are committed to social justice embarked upon an epic journey several decades ago. It has been, and continues to be, hard work, requiring much more than just soft skills. We are faced with an intricate and delicate puzzle that demands leadership, diplomacy, vision, endurance, patience, and fortitude. Having strategic business skills is not enough; getting diversity management right is a fine balance of leadership and participative governance.

Confusion about the diversity management agenda and what it seeks to achieve

Diversity management has a long-standing history of focusing on equal opportunities for certain historical minority groups. This focus has created opportunities for individuals who are members of those groups protected by anti-discrimination legislations, for example women, minority ethnic groups, people with disabilities, etc. This singular focus within an organization can been seen as contentious and divisive, as creating an unfair advantage, or as setting up different standards of behavior or performance for certain protected characteristics, such as women, people with disabilities, people from minority ethnic groups, etc.

This often results in a lack of buy-in to the legitimate rights of minorities to be on the receiving end of affirmative action (in a United States of America construct) or positive action (in a United Kingdom construct). This is a difficult reaction, particularly when people who belong to a historically privileged group, legitimize inequalities and de-legitimize the differences between them and those who have been less advantaged and underprivileged.

Organizations that do not properly communicate the reasons, and the needs, for this equalities approach, are running the risk of creating a culture of perceived exclusion and favoritism. This can result in fractious internal employee relations, and an overall dissatisfaction with an organization's diversity management position. In order to avoid this, it is essential that the leaders within an organization have a fully-formed holistic approach to diversity management, an approach that balances out the needs of all individuals while, at the same time, addresses the unique circumstances of those for whom equity and social justice has not been achieved.

In addition, diversity discomfort, the inability to speak openly and freely about differences, and of how they can be of enormous benefit, remains high for many. This is especially true in environments that give weight to being politically correct. In such circumstances, it is difficult to value and to respect diversity. But, if it is not possible to value difference, then it is also not possible to create inclusive cultures. The challenge of executive leadership is to help people unpick and debunk false notions of equality, diversity, and inclusion, and to understand how to utilize and apply the concepts of diversity, and inclusion strategically and systematically.

Too little engagement

The worlds of human resources and organizational development are predicated on the importance of employee engagement. According to a Harvard Business Review report, in 2013,[1] employee engagement has become a top priority of senior executives. It is widely understood and appreciated that high levels of employee engagement yield better business performance and bolster growth. Furthermore, literature on employee engagement points to the importance of engagement in enabling organizations to be effective. There is much less research on the concept of leadership engagement, which is the key ingredient to diversity management absent for a majority of diversity management strategies.

Most companies have far from healthy levels of employee engagement. Gallup's State of the Global Workforce Report 2013[2] shows just how dire employee engagement is. Of the world's workforce, only 13 percent of employees are positively engaged, which means that up to 87 percent of the world's employees are disengaged in their work, and in their organizations. What are they doing when they turn up for work? On top of that, the same report shows that 89 percent of the world's executive leaders are disengaged. That means only 11 percent of the world's executives are engaged in their organizations.

What leads executives to believe that their organizations can be effective without their engagement and participation? Why is it that the onus is usually put upon the staff, and little responsibility and accountability finds its way into the C-Suite? Is this thinking a hangover from the traditional command and control models of managerialism that may be impeding development and progress? The traditional view of engagement is seriously flawed.

When everyone is paid by the same organization, when every individual's name is on the payroll, does that not by definition make everyone a member of the same workplace community? I have always been stupefied by how some senior executives do not see themselves as employees, and hence divorce themselves from those to whom employee engagement pertains. The C–Suite apartheid from staff must not be carried into the future; it needs to be abolished. Senior executives need to make themselves visible and accessible as individuals.

Fear among senior executives

The full willingness of senior executives and leaders to engage in diversity education, dialogs, strategy-building, and initiatives is paramount to successful and effective diversity management. They are the ones who have to lead diversity management initiatives. Doing this convincingly and effectively requires personal exposure of imperfections. This is difficult to do if there is an overwhelming fear among executives of appearing weak or losing face if they acknowledge and show different dimensions of themselves. How many senior executives are brave enough to state publicly their own personal prejudices, and the myriad of ways in which they discriminate, either explicitly or implicitly, for and against others on a regular basis? Who in their right mind would make such an admission, in climates that are insulated by fear of punishment, political correctness, and human denial?

Roger Jones articulates what it is executives are paranoid about, and the impact of these fears and their consequences. He states:

- The biggest fear is being found to be incompetent, also known as the "imposter syndrome." This fear diminishes their confidence and undermines relationships with other executives.
- Their other most common fears, in descending order, are underachieving, which can sometimes make them take bad risks to overcompensate; appearing too vulnerable; being politically attacked by colleagues, which causes them to be mistrustful and overcautious; and appearing foolish, which limits their ability to speak up or have honest conversations.
- The five top fears resulted in these dysfunctional behaviors: a lack of honest conversations, too much political game playing, silo thinking, lack of ownership and follow-through, and tolerating bad behaviors.
- Asked to think about the fallout from those dysfunctional behaviors, the executives mentioned more than 500 consequences. Those mentioned most frequently were poor decision-making, focusing on survival rather than growth, inducing bad behavior at the next level down, and failing to act unless there's a crisis.

This may well account for the lack of engagement that we see from senior executives within the context of diversity management. Fear of exposure is very real. What may happen as a consequence of it is that there is a distinct lack of senior role modeling and leadership, which in turn alienates the wider workforce, and creates cynicism and disbelief.

In many organizations, diversity and inclusion training is rolled out to middle managers and below. Senior executives, if they do not exempt themselves, will allot themselves a very small amount of time, perhaps an hour or two, to be trained as a group. Often little or no time is given to individual senior executives for their personal development. This too must change.

IN TOUCH

A flawed concept of diversity champions

There are three types of diversity champion. The first supports an idea or cause publicly. The second is an expert, a virtuoso, someone who has dedicated time and energy into a subject area, and who is adept in a chosen field. The third is a combination of the first two, someone who wields organizational power and diversity knowledge and expertise.

Many organizations fall into the trap of selecting the first type of diversity champion. They give executive and senior leaders with positional power, but little expertise, the title of diversity champion. These champions are not experts, and often are just figureheads. Their influence is symbolic rather than substantive.

Senior executives cannot be effective leaders of others if they, as leaders, have not taken the time to clarify the diversity agenda for themselves. Their lack of knowledge, clarity, and conviction transmits to others in the wider culture, making it difficult to define clear leadership and ownership of the diversity management agenda. Without this leadership and ownership it is almost impossible to effect long-term, sustainable improvements in social justice outcomes through diversity management. Their power may even block the effectiveness of diversity experts within organizations, thus making it challenging for diversity virtuosos to truly succeed in helping their organizational cultures transform.

Labeling anyone who lacks the knowledge, skills, or ability in the field of diversity management as diversity champions could be seen as a trivialization of diversity management, and as an affront to skilled experts. This is one practice of the past that has to be questioned and examined more fully.

We need more people in the C-Suite who are diversity experts and virtuosos, not just rubber-stamping champions. To be a true champion of anything requires a certain level of personal dedication of time and energy. Through this commitment, one develops knowledge and expertise that breeds excellence.

In the past, when legal compliance was the bare minimum needed to give an organization a license to operate, symbolic leadership was more acceptable. In the twenty-first century, the operating license has shifted to emphasize the equal, if not greater, importance of an organization and its leaders having moral legitimacy. Consequently, the credibility of leaders who are simply figureheads is diminished. Alongside this, the chance of the diversity management initiatives they promote having any true and sustainable impact on social justice outcomes within their organizations is also diminished. The best outcome is seen in those organizations that have diversity champions who have power and knowledge at the base of their diversity practices.

Trapped in human resources

Historically, diversity management has been primarily a human resource management practice focused upon hiring dedicated diversity professionals; improving numeric representation of minorities; providing diversity training to staff; changing marketing material to reflect cultural diversity; providing professional developmental support of the individual; and establishing external partnerships. Such efforts arguably often result in little more than tick-boxing exercises, and overlook the systemic barriers that prevent greater and sustainable positive outcomes from being achieved.

In old-school organizational models, human resources' main diversity management function was to control "employees," but not necessarily "senior executives," and to get them to behave properly (i.e. within the confines of legal requirements) in order to avoid litigation. Often, human resources' responsibility to protect organizations from industrial employment tribunals translates into creating organizational cultures of fear and trepidation, and of command and control management. Many traditional diversity management initiatives have been born out of this.

Diversity professionals working within human resources have been labeled as the "conscience of an organization." They often operate without sufficient support from senior executives, and can be found to be working in an isolated organizational silo. Diversity professionals are expected to be "in charge" of diversity without organizational diversity performance being seen as a shared agenda with all individuals across the business. With this as a basic starting point, it is highly unlikely that a diversity initiative will be a great success and highly likely that the voice and agency of the diversity professional may be muted and eventually lost.

It is ironic that the objective of equality, diversity, and inclusion is to enable all individuals to reach their human potential. More often than not, diversity professionals are put into professional situations in which they themselves do not have the power and ability to reach their potential, simply because the organizations for which they are working are not truly committed to the process of transformation. This is not the point of diversity management, and this is certainly not the expression of social justice.

Addicted to spin

Over the years, I have attended innumerable corporate conferences and awards dinners, and I am certain that I have heard the same leadership speech given by different "diversity champions" over and over again, but only slightly modified to today's zeitgeist and audiences. The same rhetoric of equality, of change, of a need for the redistribution of power continues to play the circuit. Corporate marketing and communications may have us believe that all of the words in diversity strategies, policies, charters, training events, awards dinners, and annual reports are true; some may be. But, neither these words nor the outcomes have changed significantly over time. Guileful marketing has created a scenario of "the Emperor's new clothes," leading people to believe that diversity management is more magnificent than it truly is.

In 2015, taking a sweeping glance at mainstream media, there is an inordinate amount of human pain and suffering in the world. It appears that we have arrived at a point in time where misogyny and phobias of all sorts, from homophobia to xenophobia to religious intolerance, are dominating the global airwaves, radio waves, and microwaves. Fear, hatred, suspicion, anger, isolationism, violence, and aggression, so much negative psychology that runs counter to valuing and celebrating diversity, are alarmingly prevalent on local, national, and global scales. Yet, while the world outside is raging, the harshness of its external realities seems to be kept at bay inside the corporate boardrooms and training rooms.

Starved of social justice

Historically, the United States of America has positioned itself as the bastion, the global instigator and champion of social justice and diversity management. Many societies and businesses have been focusing their attention upon an Anglo-American diversity management framework, paying close attention to minorities and their under-achievement, their underprivilege, their underrepresentation, their under-employment, their undervaluing.

While much has changed with regards to anti–discrimination legislation, little has transformed in systemic cultural practice. Somehow, the song has remained the same.

Recent global data on social justice tells us, in fact, that today the United States of America, while it may have laws in place designed to promote equality and diversity for certain social groups, for instance minority ethnic groups and women, is not an international frontrunner when it comes to social justice. It is lagging behind countries, such as the United Kingdom, in terms of protection against discrimination for members of the disabled community, the lesbian, gay, bisexual, transgendered, and other gender-identified community, the aging community, and the community of people who are economically deprived.

In the plain light of day there are contemporary pulse points of age–old, unresolved struggles around race, cultural identity, gender identity, and disability to name a few. The United States has neither overcome nor healed from its history of segregation and oppression. So why has it been so successful in exporting its diversity management framework, and why have so many countries bought it?

We need organizations with exemplary and ethical leadership. We need to scrutinize and question the core corporate motivations that lie behind diversity management activities. We must empower diversity and inclusion professionals more. We must equip them and allow them to be change agents and activists within their organizations. We have to create more democratic and ethical organizations that engage and capture the voice of all key stakeholders, and involve them in the setting of direction and governance of their organizations.

Researchers have called for a more nuanced approach to effective diversity management, and have challenged researchers and practitioners to address the inherent power struggles that exist within organizations, and to ask the difficult questions about the impact that these power struggles have on diversity management. In answer to this call, and in moving the diversity management agenda forward, I take a deep, close look at organizational and leadership ethics, and marry ethics to diversity management practice. Years of practical and research experience have led me to believe that ethical, engaged, and empowered executive leadership is at the heart of successful diversity management. Experience has also taught me that structured governance and long–term strategy are also at the heart of successful diversity management. In pulling theory and practice together, I have formulated a strategic diversity management methodology that I call the Ethical Performance Improvement Campaign (EPIC) Journey.

The Ethical Performance Improvement Campaign highlights the importance of an ethical organizational climate, and the ability to address power relations within an organization, in relation to effective diversity management. It presents a long–term, in–depth methodology to improve the diversity management performance of organizations. It is modeled around research literature in the fields of diversity management organizational equity, stakeholder engagement, complexity theory, business ethics, corporate responsibility, and moral leadership. It is designed to help researchers and practitioners collect a wide array of data, from which they can establish developmental targets, build strategies, and define appropriate initiatives to help reach those targets. Robust performance data is generated so that the impact of diversity management initiatives upon the business, teams, and individuals is measurable, tangible, and demonstrable.

First and foremost, the campaign is focused upon strengthening the ethics of an organization, and creates the opportunity for diversity experts to share their expert knowledge directly with senior executives who are the key powerbrokers within organizations.

This, in turn, enables executive leaders to work collaboratively, seamlessly, and credibly, with other key stakeholders, including diversity and inclusion professionals.

The Ethical Performance Improvement Campaign requires senior executives to make serious personal commitments to social change and social justice, and to allow for a level of social activism within themselves, their employees, and their organization, that has the potential of challenging, and even of destabilizing, status quos. Technically, that phrase means discriminating between those who are competent from those who are less competent. It is a call to action for senior executives and leaders to really step up to the plate, and to engage in ways that acknowledge their knowledge gaps, their ignorance, their insecurities, and most of all their humanity. There are several things that can be achieved with this EPIC Journey.

A big question is: "How do we know when diversity management has been effective?" One key indicator is that we see significant improvements in social justice outcomes, improvements not just for historically underprivileged and non-privileged individuals and groups, but for organizations, or for a society as a whole. Interestingly, we are then posed with a "chicken and egg" scenario. Is social justice a precursor to effective diversity management, or does effective diversity management lead to greater social justice? Either way, effective diversity management and systems of social justice are interdependent.

When it comes to social justice, every organization sits within its own wider national, cultural, political, and economic context. This wider context will shape and determine, to a large extent, the effectiveness of diversity management. The next chapter explores how certain countries perform when it comes to social justice and the Rule of Law. There is much to learn about the conditions that foster greater social justice, and what impact these conditions may have on the effectiveness of diversity management models and strategies. A global picture of social justice is presented in the next chapter, highlighting the cultures that perform best and worst in this category. It urges us to explore more closely the cultural ingredients for exemplary systems of social justice, to borrow what ingredients we can, and to apply them to our diversity management strategies in order to make them more effective in enabling organizations to achieve greater social justice through their diversity and inclusion objectives.

Notes

1 Retrieved August 14, 2015 from https://hbr.org/resources/pdfs/comm/achievers/hbr_achievers_report_sep13.pdf.
2 Retrieved August 14, 2015 from http://www.gallup.com/poll/165269/worldwide-employees-engaged-work.aspx.

2 The interminable quest for social justice

I find this in all these places I've been travelling – from India to China, to Japan and Europe and to Brazil – there is a frustration with the terms of public discourse, with a kind of absence of discussion of questions of justice and ethics and of values.

—Michael Sandel

Social justice, as we have seen throughout the centuries, is not an easy state to achieve. Many, though not all, who work in the field of diversity and inclusion fundamentally value social justice. Committed to ensuring that there is a fair distribution and use of political power, greater representation of historical minority groups within business, and that all people live free from any form of unfair discrimination, harassment, and bullying, we are in it for the long game. In order to realize these visions, we must operate within environments where the Rule of Law and social justice exist. I consider these the precursors and bedrocks of effective diversity management. Each concept, its respective global index, and its cross-cultural implications for diversity management are covered here.

It is important to set the cultural and global context of the diversity management research presented in this book. I was born in the United States of America, the birthplace of strategic human resource diversity management, but have spent all of my adult life in the United Kingdom and Europe. As both an academic and as a practitioner, I explore the effectiveness of diversity management through a biased Anglo-American lens. There is a big wide world out there, with plenty of examples of best practice, even in some of the most unexpected places. We have plenty to learn from one another.

The Rule of Law Index

The Rule of Law is an intrinsically moral notion and legal concept that is thought to symbolize an enlightened, civilized society.

The World Justice Project (WJP) has created a Rule of Law Index. The 2015 Rule of Law Index[1] measures the performance of 102 countries, and is organized around four key principles:

1 the government and its officials and agents are accountable under law;
2 the laws are clear, publicized, stable, and fair, and protect fundamental rights, including security of persons and property;

3   the process by which laws are enacted, administered, and enforced is accessible, fair, and efficient; and

4   access to justice is provided by competent, independent, and ethical adjudicators, attorneys or representatives, and judicial officers who are of sufficient number, have adequate resources, and reflect the makeup of communities they serve.[2]

The Index measures nine factors[3] and 47 sub-factors, all of which are both relevant to social justice, and required for effective diversity management within society and business. The nine factors are:

1   Constraints on Government Powers
2   Absence of Corruption
3   Open Government
4   Fundamental Rights
5   Order and Security
6   Regulatory Enforcement
7   Civil Justice
8   Criminal Justice
9   Informal Justice

Simply speaking, it prevents individuals—and, importantly, despots—from creating and imposing their own sets of laws that may infringe upon the rights and freedoms of others. It is based on the belief that law should govern a nation rather than a nation's people being governed arbitrarily by individual government administrators and officials. The Rule of Law is correlated with per capita income, and assesses living conditions and the quality of life for citizens of different countries. How is this measured?

The ethical governance standards to which government officials are expected to adhere are the very same standards that should be adhered to by leaders of business and industry. If any of these nine factors are met insufficiently, then the Rule of Law is compromised, the concept of social justice may become increasingly more distant and aspirational, and diversity management initiatives are ineffective or completely fail. This index uses a correlation of per capita income.

The Rule of Law Index scores countries between the range of 0 (lowest) to 1 (highest). The data reveals that the four top spots are held by four of the Nordic countries. Denmark ranks #1 (0.87), followed by Norway. Similar to Denmark, Norway also ranked 0.87, but because it has a lower income ranking in comparison it is ranked #2. Sweden ranks 0.85, as does Finland (ranking #3 and #4 respectively for the same reason of lower income in Finland). The remaining six top ten countries are The Netherlands (0.83), New Zealand (0.83), Austria (0.82), Germany (0.81), Singapore (0.81), and Australia (0.80), countries that all have relatively high levels of political, social, and economic stability.

The worst performing countries are Bangladesh (0.42), Bolivia (0.41), Uganda (0.41), Nigeria (0.41), Cameroon (0.40), Pakistan (0.38), Cambodia (0.37), Zimbabwe (0.37), Afghanistan (0.35), and bottom of the table, Venezuela (0.32). These territories are the most unstable and volatile, which may result in poor living conditions and quality of life for their citizens. Why is this data of interest?

First, the Rule of Law Index may provide researchers and practitioners with early indications as to which countries are most and least likely to have, or to develop, cultures predicated on the principle of social justice. In turn, we may be able to assess within which cultural contexts diversity management is most likely to exist and to be effective, and why.

I find it fascinating that while the United States of America is a global leader in diversity management, as is the United Kingdom, neither of these nations is a top ten-ranked country when it comes to the Rule of Law. Somewhere there is a weakness in the American and British governance systems that may present certain challenges for each country in achieving greater social justice and diversity within workplace cultures. Might this be because of a cultural tendency to fall into the pattern of Rule by Law, instead of Rule of Law? There is a key distinction that must be made between the two.

With the Rule of Law, the government serves the laws. Conversely, Rule by Law is a very different cultural ethos. It is one where the government uses law as the most convenient way to govern, or even control, its citizens, while maintaining absolute authority and power above the law.

I have found that many diversity management initiatives are driven by the Rule by Law ethos. Obligation and pressure to comply with anti-discrimination legislation often catalyze diversity management training and initiatives and, indeed, are used as a useful "stick" alongside the "carrot" of greater productivity. Companies receiving punitive threats, which they then pass down to their employees, is common. Sometimes this tactic feels more like kettling and crowd containment than a commitment to employee and organizational growth and development. This often results in political correctness, fear, and suspicion of diversity, all of which detract from the overall effectiveness of diversity management practices.

Agrast et al. (2011) argue that the "Rule by Law," a reward and punishment system, is a system of positive law that fails to respect core human rights guaranteed under international law at best, and does not deserve to be called a Rule of Law system. Sorabjee,[4] suggest that Rule of Law "can be a noble steed with a good jockey in the saddle." With the Rule by Law there is no steed, just a wild horse with no saddle and no jockey.

It seems to me as though we have created a system of diversity management that is more concerned about the saddle (the laws), and less concerned about the quality of the jockeys (the leadership) in the saddle. This book aims to dismantle the system of diversity management as we know it, and to reconstruct a more effective way forward that will pave the way for nobler business leaders and true diversity champions.

The Social Justice Index

The existence of laws (de jure), and application of laws (de facto) are essential for the attainment, maintenance, and evolution of social justice within society and business. Just as the Rule of Law is a pre-requisite for effective diversity management, so too is the concept of social justice.

Social justice is defined as:

> Equality and fairness between human beings. It works on the universal principles that guide people in knowing what is right and what is wrong. This is also about keeping a balance between groups of people in a society or a community. A fair perception about race, age, gender, culture, laws, traditions, beliefs is considered

a good balance. Social justice happens when a person or group of persons do not harbor the prejudices that are detrimental to peaceful and productive relationships among individuals or groups.[5]

Schraad-Tischler (2011) asserts that social justice is a central constructive element of the legitimacy and stability of any political community. He upholds that:

> A modern concept of social justice that refers to the aim of realizing equal opportunities and life chances and offers a conceptual ideal able to garner consensus needed for a sustainable social market economy.[6]

He purports that social justice is necessary if individual citizens are to achieve their full potential within a society, and achieve self-realization. He suggests societies have a responsibility to enable citizens to participate fully within society.

The Bertelsmann Stiftung, a leading German independent think tank, has produced the Social Justice Index.[7] The most recent global report was published in 2011. It highlights variations in social justice performance among market-based democratic countries that are part of the Organization for Economic Co-operation and Development (OECD). It provides evidence of how the 31 member countries vary on the dimension of social justice.

The Social Justice Index measures six key indicators: poverty reduction; access to education; labor market inclusion; social cohesion and non-discrimination; health; and inter-generational justice. The index is based on a 10-point scale, with 10 being the highest and 0 being the lowest rating. Of these indicators, poverty prevention, access to education, and labor market inclusion are heavily weighted. Poverty prevention is most heavily weighted.

The OECD's average country ranking is 6.67. The results show Iceland at the top of the table, scoring 8.73 (curiously Iceland did not participate in the Rule of Law Index research). The rest of the Nordic countries, Norway (8.31), Denmark (8.20), Sweden (8.18), and Finland (8.06), just as we see in the Rule of Law Index, perform highest in terms of social justice. The United States of America falls significantly below the OECD average, scoring 5.70 and ranking 27/31, just above Greece, Chile, Mexico, and Turkey. The United Kingdom scores a moderate 6.79 and ranks 15/31, which is just above average ranking of 6.67.

Based on overall ranking, the Nordic states (the top five) are most exemplary. Significantly lower rankings for the United States of America and the United Kingdom suggest there is some cause for concern, with a much more serious and significant concern for the United States of America.

When we split the data out, and focus on social cohesion and non-discrimination, the United States of America performs better, but still not brilliantly. It ranks 16 out of 31, lagging behind Nordic countries, Canada and Australia, and a host of Western European countries.

The picture gets worse when we split the data to reveal the United States of America's ranking on poverty reduction, the most heavily weighted indicator. The United States of America is dangerously close to falling off the bottom rung of the poverty reduction ladder, ranking 29 out of 31, ahead of only Chile and Mexico. For a market-based, democratic "super-power," this is alarming. Something is seriously wrong. The United Kingdom is just above average, reflecting a level of consistency with its aggregated score of 15 out of 31. The Nordic countries (Norway, Sweden, Finland, and Denmark) are in the top ten. As poverty is heavily weighted in the Social Justice Index, the success of the Nordic countries may be helped by them having universal welfare states that contribute to very low poverty levels within their countries.

Clearly and unequivocally, across all social justice indicators, Nordic countries have the most highly functioning societies. They govern themselves well according to the Rule of Law, and this may contribute to better social justice outcomes. At the time of writing this book, they appeared to be more egalitarian and equitable than other countries, and demonstrate that the values of equality, integration, and community are deeply rooted. This can be seen in three distinct areas: their comprehensive social policy; institutionalization of social entitlement (social rights); and their belief in the inter-dependence of the members of society.

The social justice success of Nordic countries and their cultures can be summarized by them having participatory societies that activate and enable citizens. Unlike many practices seen in other socio-political systems, Nordic states successfully combine social justice and market efficiency. They have achieved high levels of social justice and equality among their citizens. Similar strides have not been made so systematically in other cultures. It raises questions: "What can Nordic countries teach other countries that will help others to improve their national social justice outcomes?" "If these Nordic lessons are taught can the information be learned and assimilated into other cultural contexts?"

Businesses are situated within wider national contexts. There are key cultural differences in the Rule of Law and social justice performance that should be taken into account when addressing the effectiveness of diversity management in global territories. Global diversity management strategists, leaders, and practitioners may benefit greatly by taking these differences into consideration, and by scrutinizing them closely.

As diversity management has evolved into a global exercise for many multinational companies, it is important to have a clear understanding of if, how, and where social justice fits into a country's fabric. This may give us invaluable information that we can use in designing, executing and ensuring more effective global diversity management strategies.

Cross-cultural implications for diversity management

Diversity management as a strategic human resource management practice originated within the United States of America, which I refer to as having an Anglo-American framework. Yet the Rule of Law and Social Justice indices show that it is not the best role model in either category. It does not have its own house in order. So why is its diversity management framework still so dominant within the global economy?

Alarm bells should be sounding about the effective application of an Anglo-American led model of diversity management within an international context. Non-Anglo-American cultures, that have very different socio-economic and political frameworks, have a lot to contribute to the development of effective diversity management. Yet the "wholesale export" of Anglo-American models of diversity management may be preventing them from doing so. This complex dynamic may have an impact on the diversity management effectiveness within particular cultural contexts.

For instance, in some circumstances multinational corporations may be operating in territories with no anti-discrimination legislation, and where the Rule of Law is low. In such cases, corporations cannot be reliant upon the pressure of legal compliance. What can they do to protect employees and other key stakeholders, and to promote social justice, not just within an Anglo–Saxon context, but within contexts that make cultural sense and have cultural legitimacy for non–Anglo–Saxon cultures?

In other circumstances, multinational companies may be operating in territories that rank more highly than the United States of America and the United Kingdom on the Rule of Law and social justice indices. In such circumstances, do Anglo–American multinationals companies leave enough room for themselves to learn from these cultural territories, and how socio-political and economic constructs with higher-ranked countries can contribute to improving social justice outcomes and ultimately more effective diversity management?

These questions provide an interesting backdrop to discussions of diversity management, particularly as most diversity management initiatives originate from the United States of America. The United States of America appears to lack effectiveness within its own cultural context. Introducing and applying its concepts of social justice and diversity management within foreign territories may be extremely detrimental to establishing and developing social justice and diversity management within those territories.

The data show that there are countries with more admirable, more democratic systems of governance than the United States of America. If we continue to use the American framework of diversity management as the baseline for global diversity management and practice, then we may be destined for eternal mediocrity at best.

Diversity management frameworks that are solely reliant upon the Rule of Law, and a compliance-based approached, invariably have very limited global efficacy. The next chapter will explore three sometimes competing, diversity management approaches, all of which I believe need to operate simultaneously, and work together seamlessly, in order to increase the effectiveness of diversity management practices and to achieve better social justice outcomes.

Notes

1 Retrieved July 1, 2015, from http://worldjusticeproject.org/methodology.
2 Retrieved July 1, 2015, from http://worldjusticeproject.org/what–rule–law.
3 Retrieved July 1, 2015, from http://worldjusticeproject.org/factors.
4 Retrieved July 1, 2015, from http://www.newindianexpress.com/columns/soli_j_sorabjee/ Rule-of-law-should-not-be-confused-with-rule-by-law/2013/09/22/article1796377.ece.
5 Retrieved July 1, 2015, from http://socialjusticedefinition.com/.
6 Retrieved July 1, 2015, from www.sgi-network.org/pdf/SGI11_Social_Justice_OECD.pdf.
7 Retrieved July 1, 2015, from www.sgi-network.org/pdf/SGI11_Social_Justice_OECD.pdf.

3 Vying for attention

Competing diversity management discourses

> Different roads sometimes lead to the same castle.
> —George R.R. Martin, *A Game of Thrones*

In market-based economies, it is a dog eat dog world. Competition is everywhere. We can even find it within the field of diversity management. There are three distinct, and sometimes competing, diversity management discourses: equality, diversity, and inclusion. These discourses are often blurred together and misunderstood in theory and in practice. This confusion breeds a certain lack of clarity about what diversity management is, what it seeks to achieve, and how best to achieve it.

Before exploring the wide body of diversity management literature, I would like to define these three prevalent diversity management discourses. This will help clarify and contextualize the basis of the theories and practices that I examine more fully later on in the book.

The equality framework

The ultimate aim of the equality framework is to improve social justice outcomes for underrepresented or socially disadvantaged groups. Equality literature is grounded in the "legal case," and focuses upon the drafting and application of anti-discrimination legislation, and the application of the Rule of Law. The definition of equality put forward by Skills for Business is as follows:

> *Equality* is the current term for "Equal Opportunities." It is based on the legal obligation to comply with anti-discrimination legislation. Equality protects people from being discriminated against on the grounds of group membership i.e. sex, race, disability, sexual orientation, religion, belief, or age. Equality protects people from minority groups, and those associated to people from minority groups, from being discriminated against on the grounds of group membership.[1]

This framework ensures that all groups and individuals are treated the exact same, and have access to the same level of resources and opportunities. It is a construct that is driven by legal compliance, and which often uses punitive measures as an incentive to encourage companies to comply legally.

In the United Kingdom, laws are designed to protect all people from being discriminated against within employment, education, the provision of goods and services, and access to public facilities. It has a special place within employment law, giving employees of a business protection from unfair treatment, and recourse to justice through employment tribunals.

Diversity management has historically been based upon the Rule of Law, depending heavily upon compliance with anti-discrimination and human rights laws as they apply within different jurisdictions. There are significant cultural differences when it comes to legal structures even within Anglo-Saxon cultures, such as the United States of America, the United Kingdom, and some Northwestern European countries.

This legalistic, compliance-based framework provides companies with a legal structure within which they can operate, and represents the bare minimum of what is acceptable. Many companies stop at this, and explore no other discourses, or motivations with regard to encouraging diversity and social justice.

The equality framework in isolation can give rise to reactionary and defensive organizational cultures that use the fear of punitive damages in order to get people to behave in accordance with the law. While legal compliance is indeed a basic civility, as a standalone approach it can give breath to cultures based upon political correctness and lacking humanity and morality.

Legal mandates are necessary to provide a framework of acceptable social behavior, however, mandates alone, particularly those based upon a deficit model, are insufficient for ensuring effective management of diversity within organizations (Kochan et al. 2003). One key concern with an equality framework is that, historically, within many societies, a prevalent and socially acceptable belief has been, and in some cases still is, that certain groups (for example, women, disabled people, members of certain ethnic groups, lesbian, gay, bisexual, and transgender people) are inherently inferior to established normative groups. This is known as cultural deficit theory.

Based upon this theory, individuals and their groups do not and cannot achieve certain levels of social status within society due to their deviance from the norm, without some form of intervention to increase their ability and acceptability. Social, political, and economic inequality are seen as "natural" consequences of the "natural" inferiority of certain groups. Very often, there is a high expectation that those who deviate from the cultural norm should assimilate, and understanding and valuing cultural diversity often remains low.

The cultural deficit theory is referred to extensively in literature on teaching and learning in education. Below is a statement made within this context; it is also relevant to organizational development.

> After more than two decades of federal legislation and implementation of the "deficit" model, there are now mounting concerns about the outcomes of people who have been served in this manner. Despite years of legal mandates, many individual minority group members and their groups continue to "fall through the cracks."[2]

There is a distinct disadvantage in depending upon traditional legal constructs of equality in order to stimulate and support improvements in social justice. There is an increased tendency to dismiss the agenda, and avoid its strategic business importance, if it is seen to exclusively focus upon [minority groups] (Morrison et al. 2006). Neither the equality framework nor the deficit model analyzes social, political, and environmental factors and practices that may give rise to social injustice.

Within cultural deficit theory, social minority groups are seen as deficient, and often as detracting from value. In order to counter this negative view of culturally diverse peoples, the concept of "valuing" diversity emerged in the 1990s. This was a response to unsatisfactory levels of social justice reached within an equalities framework.

The diversity framework

In the 1990s, the concept of valuing diversity arose from the equality tradition, and changed the language of diversity management from one of legal compliance to profit maximization. Financial arguments were developed to appeal to executives in the C-Suite, particularly chief financial officers who hold the purse strings, in order to motivate executives to invest their organization's money on diversity management initiatives.

Convincing arguments were developed, and data has been generated to back them, showing that fair and socially just organizations will reap a significant return on their investment in staff and organizational development. At this point, we saw a distinct shift from organizational behavior being motivated by legal compliance to being motivated by profit maximization. We went from an equality discourse, where it cost organizations money by them behaving badly, to a diversity discourse where companies can make more money by behaving justly.

It challenges the deficit model by suggesting those who are culturally diverse add value to business and society. Skills for Business defines "diversity" as follows:

> [Diversity refers to] a wide range of conditions and characteristics. In terms of businesses and their workforces, it is about valuing and reaping the benefits of a varied workforce and making the best of people's talents whatever their backgrounds. Diversity encompasses visible and non-visible individual differences. It can be seen in the makeup of the workforce in terms of gender, ethnic minorities, disabled people, etc., about where those people are in terms of management positions, job opportunities, and terms and conditions in the workplace.[3]

The main aim of diversity management is to maximize profit by fully engaging a diverse range of employees and customers, by clearly demonstrating value for cultural differences.

Workforce 2000 (Johnston and Packer 1987) moves diversity management rhetoric from discussions of bare minimum compliance with equal opportunities laws (equalities), to seeing diversity as an added value to business proposition. Effort was put into linking diversity with improved financial performance outcomes. This has come to be known as the business case for diversity.

On the basis of *Workforce 2000*, diversity management practices began to focus upon changes in United States of America demographics, and assert that businesses must begin to value diversity if they are to capitalize upon the talents and buying power diverse peoples bring to the marketplace. It is argued that diversity will help increase creativity, productivity and, ultimately, profitability. This quickly became an attractive idea within a growing global marketplace in which cultural diversity is high. Cultural diversity awareness and cultural competence became management competencies that some companies integrated into their performance reviews.

The diversity framework implicitly supported equality's anti-discrimination position; it also expanded and applied anti-discrimination to social groups not protected by legislation. This includes characteristics such as social class, personal learning styles, lifestyle choices, and other individual and group differences.

This framework suggests that valuing diverse groups and individual differences yields better business results and improves financial bottom line performance. Today, there is widespread agreement among researchers that there is a dearth of empirical evidence to support the business case for diversity. Overall, this field of research is seen to be lacking in sophistication, breadth, and depth (Curtis and Dreachslin 2008). But it could also be true that very little, if any, empirical data has been generated presenting a compelling and real business case for diversity.

Researchers have explored links between diversity and improved financial performance, and have found none; they now call for a modification of the business case. I am not saying that there is no connection. But, what I am suggesting is that there are more factors that we have to take into consideration which determine how effective diversity can be for business. I agree with my fellow researchers that the business case for diversity currently in place, and adopted by many organizations, is based upon too simplistic a model. What is needed is a more nuanced view that focuses on conditions that leverage benefits from diversity (Kochan et al. 2003:17).

The inclusion framework

Inclusion, in its true essence for me, is about giving a variety of people freedom of expression and the power to influence and change status quos, particularly when status quos are unfairly discriminatory, and/or lacking in creativity and insight. The main aim of the inclusion agenda is to value people regardless of their social groupings. Jayne and Dipboye (2004) define inclusion in the following statement:

> Inclusion as a diversity strategy attempts to embrace and leverage all employee differences to benefit the organization and individual. As a result, managing all workers, not just those representing social minority groups, becomes the focus of the diversity initiative. Inclusion broadens the scope beyond legally protected characteristics to include a much larger and wide-ranging pool of individual differences.
>
> (p. 410)

Both diversity and inclusion frameworks advocate fairness for all individuals and groups, regardless of social categorization. This framework focuses on the individual and has thus been criticized because of its tendency to de-politicize social injustice, and because of the persistent discrimination against certain groups within any given society. It has not been well looked upon by advocates of the equality framework, who are focused upon anti-discrimination and removing historic institutional barriers that create and perpetuate social injustice.

The inclusion framework, however, does not have to been seen as either a departure from, or an avoidance of institutional inequity and discrimination. I define inclusion in terms of including all individuals, and groups, in decision-making processes, in the shaping and in the governing of organizations. I see it as a state in which we can value, respect, and learn from the views and experiences of other people that differ from our own, even in the face of disagreement. It is a key ingredient for active participation engagement, and for the creation of accordance.

I believe that one key reason for the failure of diversity management initiatives is the perceived stakeholder inequity of diversity initiatives; initiatives are often seen as exclusively for the benefit of underrepresented groups. In this book I want to adopt a more inclusive approach to diversity management, one that has the capacity to engage all stakeholder groups and interested individuals in the change processes of diversity management initiatives. This is an attempt to minimize the perception of the illegitimacy, exclusion, and disadvantaging of majority groups.

A balanced and informed approach to diversity management comes from having an integrated understanding of the inter-relationship and the inter-dependence, between all three frameworks. We need to discern when to apply the appropriate framework, or frameworks, given particular conditions. None of the models fits all circumstances. Having defined the three competing discourses, I will now explore more fully the history of diversity management and ways in which we can build upon this body of literature in order to inform and improve the strategic development of diversity management theory and practice.

Notes

1 Retrieved July 1, 2015, from www.sfbn-equality-diversity.org.uk/meaning.html.
2 Retrieved July 1, 2015, from http://elearndesign.org/modules/ocada603_acn1/15/glossary/defici05.html.
3 Retrieved July 1, 2015, from www.sfbn-equality-diversity.org.uk/meaning.html.

4   Conquering diversity inertia

> I believe that movements to suppress wrongs can be carried out under the protection of our flag.
>
> —Mary Harris Jones ("the grandmother of all agitators")

Global diversity management practice is in a state of arrested development. The purpose of diversity management is to effect social change and to improve social justice outcomes, particularly for vulnerable groups within society. In practice, this does not always happen. This chapter reviews diversity management literature within strategic human resource management. It reveals where and why diversity management practices have not been as effective as they could be. It explores how we, as researchers, practitioners, and people who care deeply about justice, can improve our theoretical approach to diversity management in order to improve practical, meaningful, and sustainable social justice outcomes. It also looks at diversity training, and the shortcomings in its practice. In addition, in an attempt to create a clearer and more complete picture of what can help us be more effective, a broad body of literature, relevant to but somewhat neglected by traditional diversity management research, will be reviewed. This includes: organizational equity; complexity theory; stakeholder engagement; corporate responsibility; business ethics; and moral leadership.

After over 40 years of civil rights and anti-discrimination legislation in the West, while notable progress has been made in the areas of equality, diversity, and inclusion, citizens living within and without democratic market-economies continue to experience significantly high levels of discrimination, harassment, bullying, exclusion, and inter-group conflict. This continued concern has functioned as a call to action for me, and has spurred me to dig deeper into what might be missing in, or removed from, our diversity management thoughts and actions.

Women are still facing obstacles in career progression, particularly in long-hours work cultures. Equal pay for women doing the same job as men, in reality, is just as far out of reach, if not more, as it was in the 1970s. People with mental health illnesses continue to be stigmatized, demonized, and ostracized. Economically disadvantaged groups are caught within poverty cycles and downward spirals. The list goes on. On the basis of this, how effective has diversity management been?

For every protected characteristic, under national and international law, there is some form of discrimination that still needs to be addressed. Yet, we have beautifully crafted laws that say none of this should be happening, and upon which we have built our diversity management frameworks and practices. Clearly we have gotten many things right, but we have also gotten many things wrong. Our errors are not only creating inertia, they are harming our overall diversity management mission of creating greater fairness and social justice within society and business.

The fact that diversity has to be "managed" raises questions about what is really going on here. It suggests that diversity is something that must be controlled, like a mob that could spiral into chaos. To have to manage diversity smacks of the command and control style of management, where something has to be contained and manipulated in order to ensure a smooth running of the corporate machine. The title "diversity management" may create a feeling of restriction in some people.

Who is it that has to be managed and how? Who is supposed to be managing them? Is diversity management a strategy designed by the powerful for the powerless to remain powerless? Is it a ruse that enables businesses to be seen to be doing something, without having to demonstrate an ability to make substantial and fundamental changes to the status quo and the power structure that has bred inequality? These are some of the tougher questions, some of the more critical questions, that have often been avoided or skirted around.

Past diversity management research has done very little to help researchers and practitioners understand the key institutional barriers that may preclude effective diversity management, and to provide an educational curriculum to enable each person to develop a greater understanding of their own biases and the impacts they have on society. It has yet to explore barriers that may be instrumental in maintaining organizational status quos resistant to equality, diversity, and inclusion, and that consequently may block improvements in effective diversity management and business performance outcomes. We cannot afford to continue denying how ineffective, and at times counterproductive, diversity management practices have been.

Discrimination and bullying are often inextricably linked and result in poor workforce morale and performance. Morale refers to a mental and emotional state. When it is low, it is difficult to perform effectively. Many organizations and researchers acknowledge the detrimental impact that poor morale has on their business operations.[1] *Dismantling Diversity Management* takes a big leap in proposing that businesses, given the incredible complexity of the world's social, economic, and political fabric, must embrace morality to improve morale, and not just seek to act merely for reasons of legal compliance or profit.

It presents a joined-up system of leadership and governance that extends beyond human resources into the wider fields of business ethics, organization development, and leadership development. The book emphasizes the vital importance of activating values-driven, inclusive leadership, and of living, not just stating, corporate values. It also considers some of the key flaws in traditional diversity management thinking, looking at two central questions:

Which institutional factors within an organization's cultural environment prevent and promote effective diversity management?

and

How can social justice outcomes be improved by strengthening the ethical performance of senior executive teams, and by applying a system of participative governance based on the principles of ethical leadership equality, diversity and inclusion?

In *Dismantling Diversity Management* I critique how some corporate structures may have co-opted people into a diversity management model that perpetuates, rather than transforms, the status quo. I provide a roadmap of how to break this ineffective cycle, and of how, strategically and operationally, to embed the value of diversity into core business functions, in order to improve employee engagement and social justice outcomes.

The shortcomings of diversity training

In the 1990s, diversity management became a significant strategic human resource activity. By the twenty-first century, most Fortune 500 companies had embraced diversity management, and had begun to introduce diversity initiatives into their organizations. In 2002, 75 percent of Fortune 1000 companies boasted some sort of diversity initiative (SHRM and Fortune 2002[2]). At this time, diversity training tended to be the first and only initiative undertaken by companies.

There are numerous areas of employment upon which diversity management initiatives are focused, and that warrant research and consideration. The most common areas of activities are: leadership; research and evaluation; recruitment; retention; professional development; corporate communications; external partnerships; training; staffing and infrastructure (Jayne and Dipboye 2004).

Of these activities, diversity training is predominant. It has been a key organizational response to the pressure to comply with anti-discrimination legislation. In theory, diversity training should encourage employees to value the physical, cultural, and interpersonal differences that proponents of diversity argue enhance decision-making, problem-solving, and creativity at work. This is a good thing, but all too often this training is a stand alone response to human resource training requirements, dislocated from strategic plans of action, and does not deliver its promised goods.

In 2003, the diversity training industry was estimated to be an $8 billion industry (Hansen 2003; Anand and Winters 2008). Unfortunately, however, studies have found diversity training rarely leads to desired long-term changes in attitudes and behavior. As Kochan et al. state:

> employee participation in diversity-education programs had limited impact on performance ... Participation in diversity-education programs did not foster a positive relationship between racial and gender diversity and performance. It had no impact on racial diversity-performance link, and unexpectedly, a negative impact on the gender diversity-performance link for one measure of performance.
>
> (Kochan et al. 2003:12)

This is a major concern, leading many to believe that diversity training is a misguided practice.

To add to this, *Training's* 2005 Industry Report revealed that 71 percent of companies provided diversity and cultural awareness training for their employees (Curtis and Dreachslin 2008:108). Research into diversity management shows interventions do not yield measurable benefits at employee, team, or organizational level (Dreachslin et al. 2004:968; Roberson et al. 2001:872; Sanchez and Medkik 2004:517). This required an extraordinary amount of expenditure. The evidence prior to this level of spending clearly would have advised against it. So why did companies continue to spend such exorbitant amounts of money on something that was not going to be effective in improving social justice outcomes?

It is hard to see any significant return on its investment, especially in a country like the United States of America, given that in 2011 it ranked 27th out of 31 countries on the Social Justice Index, and that not a lot has improved since then. Is this expenditure an exorbitant waste of resources, given the time, the energy and money spent? Or is it money well invested as a part of damage limitation? There is a distinct difference between investing in improving social justice outcomes versus investing to limit damage to finances and to reputation. The latter promotes growth and progress while the former just stops things from getting worse without yielding any true signs of improvements.

Why then does this corporate practice continue? This begs the question "When introducing diversity management, and its initiatives, do organizations really aim to transform themselves?" If an organization's motivation to engage in diversity management remains ignoble, and is merely based upon a punitive thinking and behavior, then its diversity management initiatives may do more social, economic, and psychological harm than good. We are reminded that, in order for an organization to govern according to the Rule of Law, what is required are noble steeds (organizations) and the good jockeys (leaders) with the will and the capacity to enable their organizations and their societies to improve social justice outcomes for individual employees and other stakeholders.

Institutional power plays and the lack of organizational equity

There are real institutional barriers that prevent diversity management from being effective. Diversity management has limited effectiveness if the people responsible for it within an organization have little or no political power. Human resource professionals have been the primary architects, initiators, and custodians of diversity management practices. A primary function of human resources today is to protect the organization, not the human resources upon whom the organization is dependent, and who may feel at times as though they are unfairly treated. Human resources does not exist to support an employee-led movement of social justice, which one can argue is a true purpose of diversity management, within the organization.

Historically, initiatives have often stood alone, isolated from core business concerns. This has improved over time, as human resources as a discipline has created human resource business partners. Nonetheless, diversity management initiatives are often seen as little more than box-ticking exercises to exonerate organizations and their executives from any wrongful acts of discrimination committed by their employees.

Zanoni and Janssens (2007) have created a theoretical relational model of diversity management that highlights key factors that lead to micro-emancipations, defined as a myopic focus on small-scale struggles and fundamentally ignoring many of the broader social struggles that challenge management. Their assertion is that employees are controlled by a specific mix of bureaucratic and discursive controls. I believe diversity management placates employees with small changes, and to a large extent avoids making fundamental changes in the organizational status quo. This, in turn, results in diversity management practices that do little to overturn institutional inequity, and improve social justice outcomes.

They see diversity management primarily as a source of employee control, where employees are co-opted into a system in which they have no ability to challenge the underlying power relations and status quo responsible for having created the initial and deep-seated inequities. What keeps them engaged in the process is the achieving of micro-emancipations.

Over time, the demand for organizations to manage diversity proactively has become too big an ask. Consequently, organizations have recruited dedicated diversity and inclusion professionals to be the good jockeys. They have historically been located within human resource teams. The diversity and inclusion professional, often defined informally as "the conscience of the organization," has been placed in organizational diversity management saddles, often with full responsibility for organizational practice, but with very little voice and agency to have a real impact upon executive leadership practices and organizational culture.

In many instances, diversity professionals are given lofty titles, but no real authority or power to challenge the status quos they are hired to change. While organizations create diversity professionals, the organizational regimes of inequality starve diversity and inclusion professionals of strategic resources, and place barriers in front of them preventing them from effecting social change within their organizations (Tatli and Özbilgin 2009:254). There are real power plays within diversity management, which to date have not really been unearthed and exposed. Contemporary researchers also argue that the agency and voice of diversity professionals within organizations must be scrutinized.

Whether diversity professionals are positioned with a high level of prestige and influence plays a crucial role in the agency of diversity managers. Lack of, or heightened, status can either hinder or encourage their actions (Tatli and Özbilgin 2009:249). The success of diversity initiatives cannot be achieved in the absence of systemic support of diversity professionals. Are diversity professionals equipped and meant to succeed? Or are they, like human resources, organizationally designed to protect the organization and its executive leadership from damages, and not to support transformational culture change?

The power and influence that diversity and inclusion professionals either possess or lack is significant in framing our understanding of diversity management's effectiveness. One person should not single-handedly be given full responsibility for an agenda that cuts across the whole of each business, and touches every single person within a business and its external stakeholders. If diversity management is going to be genuine, if it is going to be effective in improving social justice outcomes, then it requires structural business mechanisms of support and multi-stakeholder engagement (Tatli and Özbilgin 2009:253).

Future research should take into account the influence of individuals and collective agency (stakeholder engagement) within an organization. The research conducted for this book explores the competencies of a diversity manager, collective agency, and organizational socio-political contexts.

> If diversity research is to overcome the limits of its managerial roots and promote practices that truly value differences within equality, it will need to address critically the role of power in the construction of difference and its managerial use.
>
> (Zanoni 2004:72)

While this book emphasizes the importance of strategic human resource management as an essential part of strategic diversity management practices, it asserts that diversity management practices will continue to be rendered ineffective if there is no fundamental shift in the managerial power structure of command and control, and domination. The integration of diversity objectives throughout different key business functions, not just human resources, and executive ranks within an organization, plays a crucial role in determining the effectiveness of diversity management strategies and initiatives, as does the active involvement of all stakeholder groups in the mainstreaming of diversity management and improving its outcomes.

Research exploring the effectiveness of diversity management should take into full consideration organizational conditions under which such diversity management is executed. Organizational status quos that create inequalities between groups and individuals, as well as the quality of leadership within organizations, must be more closely scrutinized. The political nature of organizational change processes and the oversimplification of the role and capacity of change agents should not be overlooked (Tatli and Özbilgin 2009:247).

Some literature suggests that organizational (workplace) equity is a pre-condition for any successful diversity management initiative. This suggests that corporate governance structures and the quality of leadership and management may have some influence upon outcomes of diversity management initiatives.

Curtis and Dreachslin (2008) remark:

> There is consensus in the literature that effects of demographic diversity are dependent on leadership, culture and climate, and organizational strategy, with external strategy and an innovative culture being associated with success in leveraging diversity for financial advantage (Gilbert & Ivancevich 2000). Providing a supportive organizational context is essential to success. Merely changing workforce demographics without properly designed organizational development interventions will likely produce more harm than good (Kossek et al. 2003). In addition, organizations need effective team processes to make diversity policies and practices successful (Ely 2004:s130).

This is a very important conceptual development. It emphasizes the need to explore and to unravel forms of institutional inequality and discrimination that may disadvantage social minorities with characteristics protected by legislation, and a wider variety of stakeholders, including members of demographic social majority groups. Addressing organizational equity, rather than equality of demographic groups, may make it more difficult for such organizations to dismiss the importance of equality, diversity, and inclusion.

Lumby et al. (2005) highlight:

> Few case study providers saw a moral or business imperative to consider diversity management. Moreover, external requirements to collect data on representativeness appear to be deflecting organizations from deeper engagement with diversity.

If we are going to make improvements in this field, then it is essential that managerialism and human resource management should not be the dominant frameworks that guide diversity management and social justice.

Complexity theory

Diversity is complex. It is possible to argue that diversity management practices are ineffective due to the inability of businesses to really grapple with the complexities that arise through diversification. Indeed, Strike et al. (2006) assert that "firms act irresponsibly because it is difficult to manage [the] increased complexity that comes with international diversification." It is essential, therefore, to understand and apply principles of complexity theory to organizational development in order to improve social justice performance.

Complexity theory can be defined as:

> the measure of heterogeneity or diversity in internal and environmental factors such as departments, customers, suppliers, socio-politics and technology.
>
> (Amagoh 2008:1; Mason 2007)

Human resource definitions of diversity have come to refer to social categories of people. This is, however, a bastardization of diversity's historic meaning. Diversity, according to its original definition in the English language, is synonymous with variety.[3] With variety comes complexity.

Complexity theory enables individuals and organizations to re-examine how diversity is understood. It helps to broaden the debate beyond equality and multiculturalism. It enables social actors to look more closely at the implications and outcomes of systems based upon command and control (the traditional legislative approach to equality and diversity), versus systems in which all social actors work together to create desired outcomes, and make judgments and act upon those judgments based upon what they feel is best, not based simply upon what is legislated.

It is argued here that many diversity management programs may have failed because leaders and practitioners have failed to gain the skills needed to manage complex organizational systems effectively. Diversity training may be inadequate because it only focuses on demographic diversity and inter-group relations, rather than on systems-thinking and how to manage complex organizations. Complexity theory, therefore, offers valuable insights that may be instrumental in improving diversity management theory and practice within organizations.

Morrison (2010) argues:

> Complexity theory [CT] suggests that leadership emerges through interactions, networking, and connectivity and relationships, as these enhance operational effectiveness. Leadership and management, from the perspective of CT, is adaptive, participative and enabling (Schreiber and Carley, 2006). On the one hand, this advocates distributed leadership that operates in ever-changing and unpredictable environments, and, on the other hand, it suggests employee empowerment, voice, creativity and diversity have considerable significance.
>
> (p. 375)

The Diversity Quality Cycle that I will present is modeled after the principles of complexity and employee engagement. In my experience of diversity management practices, employee engagement has been primarily in the form of membership of network groups, such as multicultural networks, disability networks and lesbian, gay, bisexual, and transgender networks.

These employee networks, while designed to increase the value of diversity, are built upon the foundations of an equality framework, as groups are primarily formed around underrepresented groups; this is not an inclusive approach to diversity management. The Diversity Quality Cycle's main contribution to knowledge and practice is that it presents an inclusive form of employee engagement that transcends traditional diversity network groups, and has the capacity to involve all stakeholders in integrating social justice into core business functions.

Complexity theorists, such as Mitleton-Kelly (2003), highlight the relevance of complex evolving systems that they see as essential for the process of innovation and change. Innovative organizational development happens when all actors within an organization actively contribute in the decision-making processes and actions required in order to achieve improved performance. This is referred to as "co-creating." Another essential condition of effective organizational development, according to complexity theorists, is a self-enabling environment where management is neither prescriptive nor solely top-down, and where leaders are not detached from identifying themselves on equal terms with other stakeholders.

Mitleton-Kelly (2003), in her chapter entitled "Ten Principles of Complexity & Enabling Systems," argues that in order to create new order, it is necessary to have certain organizational conditions that will allow for this. She sees these as: self-organization; emergence; connectivity; inter-dependence; feedback; far from equilibrium; space of possibilities; co-evolution; historicity and time; path-dependence. This level of theorizing provides us with a framework that supports and promotes the emergence of change, and that fosters creativity and innovation. Central to this is collective involvement of all actors within an organization in a fair and democratic manner; this proposition is concurrent with stakeholder engagement theory. The effectiveness of such an approach is explored later in this book more fully when I introduce the Diversity Quality Cycle, which is a system of collaborative and participatory governance.

Stakeholder engagement

While there is growing empirical evidence to support a connection between diversity management and organizational financial performance (the business case), there is evidence that supports a strong correlation between levels of stakeholder engagement and overall corporate performance (Lockwood 2007). An engaged employee is:

> someone who feels involved, committed, passionate and empowered, and demonstrates those feelings in work behavior.
>
> (Mone et al. 2011:206)

Freeman (1984)[4] introduced a stakeholder model. He defines a stakeholder as pertaining to "an individual or group who benefits or are harmed by, and whose rights are violated or respected by, corporate actions." His work challenges the assumption that the (financial) needs of stockholders, or as we now refer to them, shareholders, have primacy over the needs of other groups that have a vested interest in the success of a corporation. When looking at the relationship of management to stockholders, based on this assumption of primacy, management is defined as managerial capitalism. Central to his thinking, he argues that managers have a fiduciary responsibility to shareholders, and stakeholders must be active participants in their work organizations.

The stakeholder groups central to Freeman's stakeholder model of a corporation are: owners; management; local community; customers; employees; and suppliers. This model is a theoretical basis of the Diversity Quality Cycle. In the action research presented in this book, each of these stakeholder groups is engaged in the process of diversity management and the achievement of improved social justice outcomes within the main case study organization. All stakeholder groups participate actively (some more actively than others) in the change process, and on an equal footing in terms of voice and agency.

Freeman speaks specifically of corporation law, which establishes that each corporation is defined as an individual entity, and has limited liability and immorality as its key features. On the basis of this law, companies have been permitted to act in an unrestrained manner in order to maximize profits to benefits of shareholders. Corporate restraints in the form of regulation have increased over time. Within the context of diversity management, anti-discrimination laws, and human rights laws, and the duty to comply with them in labor relations has imposed restraints on corporations. The notion of corporate social responsibility becomes relevant to discussions of diversity management, and will be discussed in the next section.

Employees who are highly involved in their work processes, for example, those who conceive, design, and implement workplace and process changes, are more engaged. By definition, this is a high-performance work system. It enables employees to exercise decision-making, leading to flexibility, innovation, improvement, and skill sharing. As highlighted in the literature, the link between high-involvement work practices and positive beliefs and attitudes, as associated with stakeholder engagement and generating behaviors leading to enhanced performance, is an important driver for business success.

A report produced by the SHRM Foundation shows stakeholder engagement can be measured in dollars, and can yield significant savings. For example, at the beverage company of Molson Coors, it was found that engaged employees were five times less likely than non-engaged employees to have a safety incident, and seven times less likely to have a lost-time safety incident.

The average cost of a safety incident for an engaged employee was $63, compared with an average of $392 for a non-engaged employee. Consequently, through strengthening stakeholder engagement, the company saved $1,721,760 in safety costs in 2002. In addition, savings were found in sales performance teams through engagement. In 2005, for example, low-engagement teams were seen falling behind engaged teams, with a difference in performance-related costs of low- versus high-engagement teams totaling $2,104,823.

Research also shows customer loyalty is closely related to stakeholder engagement. In a recent empirical study (Lockwood 2007), the relationship between the availability of organizational resources (i.e. training, technology, and autonomy) and stakeholder engagement in work units was found to have a positive effect on employee performance and customer loyalty. When employees feel more engaged in their work, the corporate climate is better for service and customers receives better quality service, thus promoting customer loyalty. The practical implication is that organizations benefit demonstrably when employees are engaged. The challenge is for organizations to build workplace environments that foster a sustainable workplace environment of engagement, as this is attractive to a variety of stakeholders.

Employees with the highest levels of commitment perform 20 percent better, and are 87 percent less likely to leave an organization,[5] which indicates engagement is linked to organizational performance. This shows there is a correlation between employee engagement and strong retention rates.

This suggests that it may be possible to improve social justice performance through increased strategic stakeholder engagement. By being aware of the unique needs of diverse groups, as well as by recognizing individual differences, organizations can better understand the challenges of increased diversity in an organization's workforce, and work toward designing and implementing workplace policies and practices to engage diverse employee groups.

Diversity management strategies may benefit from applying stakeholder theory. Diversity management may be suffering from the Rule by Law, or capitalistic managerialism, the old style of commanding and controlling stakeholders, rather than actively engaging stakeholders. If diversity management strategies transform and engage stakeholders in the governance process (beyond membership to social network groups), rather than impose constructs of diversity management on stakeholders, then we may see improved diversity management outcomes. These outcomes may be measured, for instance, in employee satisfaction, recruitment, and retention rates.

Morrison et al. (2006) point out that employee cynicism about diversity initiatives has resulted in detrimental impacts upon organizational change processes. Employee disengagement with the diversity management agenda may be a consequence of negative perceptions and intentions of diversity management initiatives and weak organizational leadership. This suggests that if employee cynicism can be transformed into employee support through employee engagement, this may in turn help diversity management strategies to be more effective.

Below is a review of corporate social responsibility and business ethics literature. These areas are of particular importance to organizations as the "diversity" or social performance (which is seen as part of ethical performance) is increasingly scrutinized. This literature is of great importance because it also enables us to compare and contrast traditional and current approaches to corporate social responsibility. Historically organizations have acted voluntarily and out of goodwill; it is not an area heavily weighted down by need for legal compliance and box-ticking. But, as ethical consumerism has increased in the West over the decades, a business case for engaging in ethical behavior has also emerged. If people are unhappy with the ethics of a business they may be less likely to either buy from that business, or choose to work for that business.

Corporate social responsibility and business ethics

In the 1990s, and early part of the twenty-first century, academic business ethics emerged as part of higher education curricula within faculties of business and law. Academic business ethics displays its corporate social responsibility heritage in the peculiar constellation of concerns pervading its literature.[6] Therefore, it and business ethics, while distinct from one another, are inextricably linked. I will cover literature on both disciplines in this section, and end with an application of corporate social responsibility and business ethics to diversity management.

Whereas stakeholder theory is reviewed as relatively new, the first formal written accounts of corporate social responsibility date back to 1946. At this time it was mainly referred to as "social responsibility." This was partly due, it is believed, to corporations not yet having taken on the magnitude of power we see in today's modern organizations (Carroll 1999; Freeman 1984).

Corporate social responsibility theoreticians state that corporations have three general responsibilities to society: economic, legal, and ethical (Carroll 1999; Schwartz and Carroll 2003). The World Business Council defines corporate social responsibility as:

> the continuing commitment by business to behave ethically and contribute to economic development while improving the quality of life of the workforce and their families as well as of the local community.[7]

This definition is consistent with priorities of stakeholder engagement theory.

Boswell's (1997) definition of business ethics is:

> the application of diverse ideas about "right" and "wrong", the "good life" and the "good society" to the decisions, attitudes and behavior of people and institutions in profit-making business, and it does so in order to understand or evaluate, and to improve.
>
> (p. 105)

The definition of corporate social responsibility presented by the United States of America Department of Commerce, in its 2004 report entitled *A Manual for Managing a Responsible Business Enterprise in Emerging Market Economies*, defines corporate social responsibility as:

> A new business strategy in which companies conduct business responsibly by contributing to the economic health and sustainable development of the communities in which they operate, offer employees healthy, safe, and rewarding work conditions, offer quality, safe products, and service … are accountable to stakeholders … and provide a fair return to shareholders whilst fulfilling the above principles.[8]

It is important to note there is literature on cross-cultural approaches to corporate social responsibility based on countries such as Mexico, France, Indonesia, Bangladesh, and other Asia-Pacific countries. This literature, as did literature on the Social Justice Index and the Rule of Law Index, highlights divergent cross-cultural approaches to the field of corporate social responsibility. How it is defined and acted upon is shown to be dependent upon historical and cultural contexts of an organization (Blasco and Zølner 2010).

> These differences have spurred scholarly interest in cross-cultural differences in [corporate social responsibility] and business ethics of late. A key finding of this work is despite some similar tendencies in approaches to [corporate social responsibility] in Europe, the United States, Latin America, Asia, and Africa, important differences exist between and within countries, making it extremely difficult to generalize or to predict any significant degree of convergence.
>
> (Blasco and Zølner 2010:219)

Without going into too much depth, it is just worth noting and emphasizing how important it is to understand cross-cultural variations (diversity) across all of these theoretical management frameworks.

The seminal work on corporate social responsibility is Howard Bowen's book *Social Responsibilities of the Businessman* (1953). Bowen wrote that businesses were "vital centers of power and decision-making, and that action of these firms touched the lives of citizens at many points." Because of this influence, businesses carry with them a moral responsibility to communities they exist within. Bowen (1953) sought views of businessmen about statements that "businesses are responsible for the consequences of their actions in a sphere wider than the profit and loss statements."

At the time, 93.5 percent of businessmen agreed with this statement, thus confirming a centrality of social and moral responsibility within business. While there was little consensus about the definition of social responsibility, there was a shared focus upon economic and human resources; reference to environmental responsibility arose in the literature in the 1960s and 1970s.[9]

Early on, researchers argued corporate social responsibility must go beyond mere compliance with bare minimum legal requirements and the motivation to increase profitability for stockholders (McGuire 1963). Freeman's arguments in favor of stakeholder engagement echo this. McGuire was a strong advocate for the moral case, as he had a "concern for ethical consequences of one's acts as they might affect the interest of others." He put forward the argument that corporate social responsibility should arise out of volunteerism (which presumably stems from a sense of moral obligation), and not coercion (which presumably stems from legal and economic obligations).

In 1970, the Opinion Research Corporation conducted a poll, asking business executives or as they were referred to at the time "businessmen," if they felt "businesses had a moral obligation to help other major institutions to achieve social progress, even at expense of profitability." Two-thirds of respondents said they agreed with this premise (Carroll 1999). The literature states very clearly that corporate motivation to engage in socially responsible behavior should not be governed by the extent to which such action can be shown to be financially profitable to an organization in the short term (i.e. shareholder primacy). Carroll (1999) refers to Walton (1967) by saying: "Cost may be involved for which it may not be possible to gauge any direct measurable economic return" (Carroll 1999:273; Walton 1967:18).

In the 1970s, corporate responsibility evolved to include specific references to environmental impact, worker safety, consumer rights, and employee rights. Eilbert and Parker (1973) put forward the proposition that businesses must play "an active role in the solution of broad social problems, such as racial discrimination, pollution, transportation and urban decay." At the end of the 1970s, Ernst & Ernst (now Ernst & Young) accountancy firm generated six categories of activity into which corporate social responsibility had divided. They were, and remain largely: environment; equal opportunities; personnel; community involvement; products; and other (Carroll 1999).[10] This was later refined in the 1980s when alternative concepts emerged within corporate responsibility. They were: business ethics; stakeholder theory/involvement; public policy; corporate social performance; and corporate social responsiveness (Jones, 1995).

At this point in the evolution of the field, Wood (1991), who speaks in terms of corporate social performance, made a significant contribution to knowledge by advancing the concept of principles, processes, and policies. She defined the driving principles as legal, economic, ethical, and discretionary. The processes were defined as: reactive; defensive; accommodative; and proactive. The policies reflected: environmental assessment; stakeholder management; and issues of management.

Her focus was primarily upon outcomes of corporate social performance. She created a framework that positioned it within the broader business context, moving it away from being an isolated element disjointed from core business operations.

The concept of corporate social performance actively began to bridge the gap between corporate social responsibility and business ethics, as corporate social performance scrutinizes a corporation's actual performance (outcomes) with regards to its orientation and commitment to corporate social responsibility. Her research suggests corporate social responsibility rhetoric alone is insufficient in improving outcomes. The fulfillment of corporate social responsibility is dependent upon a company's actions that, as the old adage says, speak louder than words. However, the relationship between corporate social responsibility and corporate "spin" is a close one.

As we moved into the twenty-first century, corporate social responsibility became part of the cause-related marketing strategy of most businesses today, and closely linked to building brand loyalty and to reputation management. Those responsible for it mostly held roles within marketing and communications departments, as opposed to diversity management professionals who held roles primarily within human resource departments.

Part of marketing strategy is to differentiate one's company through its image of care and compassion for the community. But, as Brønn and Vrioni (2001) point out, "only a consistent believable contribution to a cause (or non-profit organization) can build brand image and brand equity." Anything less than sincerity in aim and purpose can breed levels of employee and customer cynicism, which may have the exact opposite effect of enhancing brand reputation (Herbig and Milewicz 1995). This dynamic is also reflected in responses to diversity management practices, where corporations are believed to be paying "lip service" to business integrity, or in other words business ethics.

There has been an increasing amount of corporate social responsibility literature critiquing the extent to which companies are actually "practicing what they preach." In their paper "Being Good while Being Bad," Strike, Gao, and Bansal (2006) provide convincing evidence of corporate social responsibility rhetoric not translating into corporate action or behavior. They appear to be the first authors to speak in terms of Corporate Social Irresponsibility, and assert that interplay between responsible and irresponsible corporate behavior confounds attempts to establish the financial benefit of being corporately responsible.

They analyzed 222 publicly traded companies between 1993 and 2003, and found that what one hand gives, the other takes away. One possible explanation as to why corporate social responsibility may appear more in symbolic rhetoric than in actual behaviors within a corporation is that substantive management is expensive, difficult, and time-consuming. Therefore, many managers may prefer symbolic mission statements (Ashforth and Gibbs 1990). In which case, a company would be demonstrating weak business ethics.

Barktus and Glassman (2008) analyzed the relationship between corporate mission statements that promoted corporate social responsibility and the way businesses managed their stakeholders. No relationship was found between organizations with mission statements that mention certain stakeholder groups (employees, customers, and the wider community) and behaviors regarding these stakeholders. Thus, they concluded that such statements were only appearing in annual reports and other forms of corporate communications, as a result of some external and/or institutional pressure to present them. This sounds like a very familiar sub-plot within diversity management.

The literature on corporate social responsibility and corporate social performance maintains that, when companies do not practice their commitment to business ethics that this undermines the perception of a company's integrity. In the absence of an ethical climate, literature posits that there is an increase in employee disengagement, retention rates drop, customer loyalty may be compromised, and overall corporate reputation damaged.

Stewart (2011) carried out some very interesting research exploring the relationship between employee perceptions of the diversity and ethical climates (independent variables) of their organizations, and employee turnover intention (dependent variable). He defines a diversity climate in two ways. The first is "the degree to which an organization focuses on maintaining an inclusive workplace"; this is a progressive definition that reflects the inclusion framework. The second is when "a firm advocates fair human resource policies and socially integrates underrepresented employees"; this is reflective of the equality and diversity frameworks. The "ethical climate" is defined as "the extent to which employees perceive their organization values and enforces ethically correct behavior."

The results of the study indicated that the "ethics" climate moderated the "diversity" climate–turnover intentions relationship. What on earth does that mean? It means that when employees perceived their work environment was strong on both accounts (i.e. had a strong diversity climate and a strong ethical climate), then turnover intention was very low. In short, employees were happier and felt less likely to want to leave their employers when they perceived their organizational cultural climate to be an ethical one.

Today, we must also bear in mind the impact that the financial crisis of 2008 has had on the global economy, and the job uncertainty that it has brought. It may well be that there is less employee turnover within companies as a result of there being a perceived scarcity of job alternatives in the market. If this is the case, then it may well be the case that many people, though they may be discontented with poor ethics within their organizations, do not feel they can take the risk of leaving the financial security of their current jobs, and will be more willing to endure what they consider to be unethical workplaces and practices.

This research is significant, because it empirically demonstrates a strong relationship between perceptions of the corporate climate with regards to diversity and business ethics, and the impact this perception has on employee turnover intention. Companies saying they wish to increase demographic representation of underrepresented groups must also consider the degree to which they have organizational cultures that demonstrate a high value for diversity and business ethics. Research shows that should these conditions be absent, employers may run a risk of low retention rates of the very groups they seek to recruit, thus counteracting the whole recruitment exercise.

Corporate social responsibility is relatively new as a formal business construct, despite the long history of many companies having practiced it for years. According to Blasco and Zølner (2010), several researchers have begun to explore root causes for such cross-cultural differences in corporate social responsibility performance. Key root causes identified include: national cultural values; different business systems and stages of economic and social development; legal systems; historical roots of government; and types of corporate governance. This literature is significant as these key variables are equally applicable to, yet historically neglected by, the field of diversity management.

Moral leadership

Moral leadership is an essential component of effective diversity management. A key dimension of this form of leader is that they are primarily focused upon being of service to others. With moral leaders there is no place for egotistical self-aggrandizement. Their objective is not to seek a following, but to lead by example in order to inspire others to be achievers. They are people driven by their values, and can occupy any position within organizational hierarchies. They are the noble steeds within the context of the Rule of Law referred to earlier.

O'Toole (1995) she defines a moral leader as thus:

> A strong, moral leader has "courage, authenticity, integrity, vision, passion, conviction and persistence. They listen to others, encourage dissenting opinion among their closest advisors, grant ample authority to subordinates and lead by example rather than by power, manipulation or coercion."

Moral leaders also have a highly developed sense of emotional intelligence and master key social skills. They work to overcome obstacles and are skilled at the art of consultation. They build consensus, navigate diversity, and establish unity. Moral leaders are the conscience (i.e. moral compass) of an enterprise or organization and the glue that holds it together.[11]

Maldonado and Lacey (2001) conducted a study of 12 leaders. Their objective was to hear the points of view of those leaders who acted in accordance with their values and commitments. These individuals were focused upon civil rights, peace, and public service to the disenfranchised. They found that moral leaders achieved several things. They were willing and able to take stands, speak out, bring out the best in other people, and follow their own moral compass. The qualities that they possessed were humility, good listening skills, personal truthfulness, and social activism to advance justice. This is how we can define the role of a diversity champion.

Bass (1985) feels moral leadership better serves the wellbeing of an organization in that they help others to see and address the real conflicts that exist between competing values, and they are willing to step in to bridge any gaps between espoused values and actual behavior. While this is often the type of leadership demonstrated by diversity and inclusion professionals, it is not seen as frequently in other executive and senior leaders.

Discussion and summary

Diversity management is focused upon improvements in social justice opportunities and outcomes for all stakeholders. The review of diversity management literature supports the argument that the legal case is insufficient to effect real change. The business case for diversity management is not thoroughly proven and may be potentially untenable. What remains is a moral argument, backed by a strong sense of moral duty to society.

The key shortcomings identified in this literature review are:

- a misleading focus upon demographic diversity, which can tend to alienate non-minority individuals and groups;
- HR acting as primary architects and custodians of diversity policy, strategy, and practice;

- previous research neglecting the role and influence of diversity managers as change agents;
- previous research overlooking the importance of organizational equity as a necessary pre-condition for enabling diversity to thrive and add value;
- the simplification of diversity management with little appreciation of complexity theory and organizational development; and
- the absence of discussions addressing wider corporate social responsibility, business ethics, and moral leadership.

Consequently, some skeptics argue that diversity management serves no purpose at all. Others are more harsh, and argue that diversity management is a control tool of managerialism that, by creating micro-emancipatory outcomes, subverts the social justice concerns of workers. In addition, they would argue that diversity management research fails to challenge the fundamental power relationship between managers and the managed, based on institutional managerial status quos of command and control, of top-down leadership at a distance that runs counter to the principles of equality, diversity, and inclusion.

From an equality point of view, while nominal progress can be cited, and attributed in part to diversity management, there is no compelling evidence that diversity management has yielded significant and sustainable changes in levels of social injustice. In addition, from a diversity and inclusion point of view, there is no convincing empirical evidence that diversity management has been effective in increasing either productivity within or profitability for businesses.

While there is evidence that there are some business benefits to diversity, it can neither be argued that diversity will always yield these benefits, nor that these benefits are only achieved through diversity. Contemporary diversity management researchers argue that power relations must be more closely scrutinized if researchers and practitioners are to find ways to make diversity management more effective.

This chapter has covered diversity management literature, as well as several other bodies of literature. Each individual area has significant relevance to the development of diversity management theory and practice. In advancing a more nuanced approach to diversity management, it is essential to attend to and integrate contributions made by theories of: complexity theory; stakeholder engagement; corporate responsibility; and business ethics and moral leadership.

Notes

1 Retrieved August 1, 2015 from www.researchgate.net/profile/Edward_Brown10/publication/280699294_Workplace_Bullying_A_Review_of_Its_Impact_on_Businesses_Employees_and_the_Law/links/55c1c1e608ae092e966860bd.pdf.
2 Retrieved August 1, 2015 from www.shrm.org/Research/SurveyFindings/Documents/Impact%20of%20Diversity%20Initiatives%20on%20the%20Bottom%20Line.pdf.
3 Retrieved August 1, 2015 from http://s3.amazonaws.com/academia.edu.documents/41846788/Harrison-Klein_2007_AMR.pdf?AWSAccessKeyId=AKIAJ56TQJRTWSMTN-PEA&Expires=1474801255&Signature=IYOhdWbCumdU040fSKJniUfVNYM%3D&response-content-disposition=inline%3B%20filename%3DWHATS_THE_DIFFERENCE_DIVERSITY_CONSTRUCT.pdf.
4 Retrieved August 1, 2015 from http://academic.udayton.edu/LawrenceUlrich/Stakeholder%20Theory.pdf.

5 Retrieved August 1, 2015 from http://media.roiinstitute.net/pdf/Department-Retention-ESMjunjul10.pdf.
6 Retrieved August 1, 2015 from http://plato.stanford.edu/entries/ethics-business/.
7 Retrieved August 1, 2015 from www.wbcsd.com.
8 Retrieved August 1, 2015 from http://ita.doc.gov/goodgovernance/adobe/bem_manual.pdf.
9 Retrieved August 1, 2015 from www.scu.edu/ethics/practicing/focusareas/business/product.html.
10 Retrieved August 1, 2015 from http://uga.academia.edu/httpwwwterryugaeduprofilespersonid443/Papers/398629/Corporate_Social_Responsibility_Evolution_of_a_Definitional_Construct.
11 Retrieved August 1, 2015 from www.globalethicsnetwork.org/profiles/blogs/what-do-you-mean-by-moral-leadership.

5   Managerialism maims

The dangers of command and control

> Mock participation in quality circles, singing the company song and wearing the company uniform solely to please the management all lead to distrust and unproductive work.
>
> —Milton Freeman

There is a lot of corporate bravado about valuing diversity. Yet, often, behind the veneer, we can find corporate structures that operate in ways that run contrary to the principles of equality, diversity, and inclusion. One such structure is managerialism, or what can be referred to as managerial conformity. It is associated with hierarchy, accountability, measurement, and tight control of an organization by those with positional power. Managerialism does not allow for opposing or alternative points of view to its management framework. This outlook runs counter to the very nature of diversity and valuing difference. It also oppresses and stifles the growth and development of individuals within such organizations. Ironically, this dynamic can be seen very clearly in the structure of the further education sector within the United Kingdom.

This corporate culture of further education colleges represents a kind of preserved, properly pickled old-school regime. It is top-down. It is command and control. It is compliance-based. It is weak on participative governance and stakeholder engagement. A close examination of these cultures creates a need to heed a warning for all organizations. It also generates a higher level of clarity as to why things are not working properly, and creates an inspiration to do better.

The perils of a compliance only approach

Statutory obligations under current legislation demand that these businesses demonstrate that they are proactive in their attempts to prevent and eradicate discrimination. Despite widespread usage of the phrase "equality and diversity" within further education, research shows there is little evidence of coherent diversity frameworks within these institutions.

Lumby et al. (2005) conducted focus groups in order to explore the position of equality and diversity. Their findings provide some indications as to why many business sectors and institutions may be progressing so slowly. It was found that:

1   Perceived pressure to consider "diversity" and "inclusion" varied from provider to provider. Variations were wide.

2   Interest in and engagement with diversity issues were weak or resisted by a substantial proportion of staff.
3   The understanding/definition of diversity was not always thought out and clearly articulated on an agreed basis, even within each provider organization.
4   Representativeness in relation to the local or national profile of the community was the most common aim, sometimes leading to a focus on "diversity" rather than "inclusion."
5   Action to achieve diversity was episodic rather than systemic, and based largely upon equal opportunities approaches.
6   Success in terms of raising learner numbers and achievement did not rest on managing diversity successfully, in all the contexts studied.

They go on to highlight:

> Few case study providers saw a moral or business imperative to consider diversity management. Moreover, external requirements to collect data on representativeness appear to be deflecting organizations from deeper engagement with diversity.

This research provides evidence to show that further education colleges are operating primarily according to an equal opportunities framework, and nothing more. This presents an enormous challenge to the sector from an organizational development point of view.

Equally, Morrison et al. (2006) comment:

> while the concept of diversity management has been introduced into private sector discourse, it remains largely absent from education. Recent educational reform discourses argue that schools, teachers and educational leaders should be responsive to cultural, racial, gender, sexual and religious diversity within their "client", student and indeed, parent and community populations.
>
> (Blackmore 2006)

Further education is at a crucial stage of its development. In terms of its orientation to equality, diversity, and inclusion, as a sector it is lagging far behind large government departments and the private sector (Morrison et al. 2006). If the education sector does not embrace the concept of valuing diversity and inclusion, then it may put itself into a perilous position, where it stands to do more harm than good should its antiquated approach of only applying the concept of equality prevail. The question arises: "Why are further education colleges so entrenched in an equalities framework?"

One answer may be that funding agencies require further education colleges to report on the achievements of certain demographic groups. The key categories are race, gender, and disability, in line with statutory obligations of public authorities. This keeps institutions and individuals entrenched within the equality discourse.

Overall, research results suggest there is a lack of a conceptual framework; a high proportion of staff resistance; a lack of clarity as to the definition of diversity; a lack of a system approach to diversity management and organizational development; and a lack of consideration of diversity management within its core business operation. Based upon these results, it would suggest there is a distinct lack of leadership and management of social justice agenda within the further education sector. If the sector, or any other sector, is to improve, then leadership and management should be a priority area of diversity management development.

Leadership and management

It is argued that the further education sector is stifled by forms of "new public management," which have been criticized for its attempt to micro-manage state provision through the excessive use of performance management and a pre-occupation with targets (Avis 2009). Government-by-target, which is somewhat similar in concept to the Rule by Law, is widely accepted to have reached its limits as a strategy.[1] While targets are still an essential part of a toolkit, setting linear improvement goals, and then pushing hard to achieve them, can no longer be the dominant principle for reforming large, partly autonomous organizations (Hargreaves 2003).

Debates continue about monitoring and target-setting in the field of equalities, with some arguing that adoption of a managerialist approach quells the radical edge of activism, and may result in minimal compliance (Mackay and Bilton 2000).

The managerialist versus the collaborative approach

Generally speaking, and beyond the further education framework alone, the managerial approach is based on a hierarchical, top-down approach that is based upon command and control. As noted by Sanderson (2001):

> In the UK, development of performance management in the context of "new public management" has been primarily "top-down" with a dominant concern for enhancing control and "upwards account-ability" rather than promoting learning and improvement.

Such an approach is a central feature of the new public management framework in operation within further education. This may not be the most appropriate approach to management within education. Their research demonstrates that a school environment for effective management of cultural diversity can be achieved through creative approaches to professional management and school governance, characterized by a collaborative management style. This is consistent with the tenets of social justice theory and complexity theory, which advocate in favor of enabling processes and active participation of all social actors in the process of creating improved outcomes.

Morrison (2010) also states that complexity theory offers much to leadership and management, and advocates for the application of complexity theory to educational environments. Morrison holds there is evidence of its value in informing and supporting effective change management.

> Leaders and managers face continuous and ubiquitous change in education, in which closer links with, and responsiveness to, the external environments of schools are constantly being required.
>
> The view of complexity theory adopted here, set out in the following paragraphs, expressly concerns such change, development, external linkage, and evolution and development. Complexity theory's conception and implementation break with stable, simple cause-and-effect models, linear predictability, and a reductionistic,

analytically atomistic approach to understanding phenomena and management. Complexity theory replaces them with organic, far-from-equilibrium, dynamical, non-linear and holistic approaches to leadership and management. Here relations and interactions within interconnected networks are important in times of turbulence and change.

(Morrison 2010:376)

The key characteristics of an organization valuing complexity theory can be identified as follows: co-enabling; co-creative; evolving; and self-organizing. Indeed, complexity theory suggests emergent, self-organized order may supersede command and control in many situations (Morrison 2010:375), which provides an opportunity for all institutions to depart from new managerialism, which is neither new nor effective when it comes to diversity management.

The application of complexity theory is therefore considered an important aspect of any theoretical and practical framework of diversity management. Such an approach offers executive leaders and managers an alternative to a linear, target-driven, top-down approach to management, which is thought to stifle the very diversity it attempts to value.

With regards to leadership and management, it may be advantageous to support leaders to understand complexity theory, and to provide them with the skills to respond effectively and ethically to constantly changing business landscapes, initiatives and government directives. This may enable institutions to be less reactionary and more proactive and even entrepreneurial, as they are challenged to be under current financial and legislative restrictions.

The demographics of leadership

For many years the private sector has sought to be reflective of the communities it serves, particularly when it comes to the distribution of power within organizations. Great attempts are being made to diversify Board members and senior managers within private sector organizations. In the private sector, social justice performance is often judged by the ability of an organization to achieve greater representation of traditionally excluded groups across the whole of its business. The same may not be said of further education, or generally of the public sector as a whole in the United Kingdom.

Historically, further education's main equality and diversity focus and discourse, has revolved around racial, gender, and disability equality, primarily focusing upon the rights of students (customers), to the near exclusion of considering the rights of staff (employees) and other stakeholders. There is little evidence to suggest further education has turned any strategic attention to diversifying its senior management. Thus, the status quo of further education is easily perpetuated, making change very difficult.

Turning attention back to the issue of leadership and management, it appears that a lack of diverse representation within staff, and in particular leadership and management, is not correlated to social justice performance in the way that it is in the private sector. Blackmore (2006) asserts:

> what's missing in policy and mainstream educational diversity management literature is a transformative discourse to *diversify management and leadership*. This position would put dominant management and leadership paradigms under the critical gaze

of "the other". It would mean considering how organizations may better address issues of student and workforce diversity within a broader conceptual framework of how schools as organizations relate to culturally diverse societies.

(Blackmore 2006:181)

Gradually this has changed, as there have been increasing moves to professionalize the teaching profession. Today, colleges have to function more like business enterprises, particularly within the current economic downturn. With this professionalization comes an increase in regulation. Equality, diversity and inclusion have begun to play central roles in the regulation of further education colleges and in the evolution of the business of further education sector. As with private sector organizations, good govern-ance is required within colleges in order to ensure corporate social responsibility and high performance on the dimension of social justice.

Further education is an area of public sector business in which there has been very little diversity management research conducted. According to Morrison et al. (2006), for them:

The intellectual challenge at the start of [their] research study … was the dearth of appropriate literature in which to ground emerging outcomes and findings, and "surface" formalized deliberations about diversity that sometimes lacked direction or commitment.

(Morrison et al. 2006:282)

The managerialist approach diametrically opposes the democratic tenets of diversity management, and may create great tensions within an institution as a consequence.

In answer to this, the next chapter outlines the Diversity Quality Cycle, a democratic and participatory governance framework, that is based on top-down and bottom-up management approaches, and is designed to achieve greater organizational social jus-tice overall. It is a model that is of use to both diversity management researchers and practitioners, offering practical guidance of how to make diversity management more effective.

Note

1 Retrieved August 14, 2015 from https://hydra.hull.ac.uk/assets/hull:12778/content.

6 The Diversity Quality Cycle

Tackling institutional barriers

Change fixes the past. Transformation creates the future.

—Unknown

After 15 years of experience within the diversity management industry, I bore witness to many organizations that were primarily interested in buying diversity training, and often lacked comprehensive strategies upon which training was based. They did not have robust governance structures in place to embed principles throughout business systems and culture, or to promote accountability and responsibility.

This became a source of concern and disquiet for me. I felt more could be done and needed to be done in order to really make strides in the area of diversity management. I felt that I could have made a stronger and long-lasting contribution to an organization's development and transformation as an in-house practitioner where I could co-create and apply a governance system that would help to assist significantly in the transformation of an organization's culture and its diversity management performance. The Diversity Quality Cycle (Figure 6.1) is what emerged.

What is the Diversity Quality Cycle?

The Diversity Quality Cycle is a framework that promotes the 3Es (ethical, engaged, and enlightened) leadership. It places values and ethics at its heart and provides leaders with an opportunity to become more enlightened about themselves, the experiences of others, and how best to create successful values-driven organizations.

It is designed to engage a critical mass of stakeholders within the process of bringing about effective diversity management both within organizations, and within their partner and community organizations. It serves as the main framework for, and vehicle of, governance and accountability that allows for strategies to be created, scrutinized, and adjusted in order to improve diversity management and its outcomes.

Central to the Diversity Quality Cycle are working groups that operate as quality circles. A quality circle is defined as a group of employees who perform similar duties and meet at periodic intervals, often with management, to discuss work-related issues and to offer suggestions and ideas for improvements, as in production methods or quality control.

The purpose of the Diversity Quality Cycle is for a variety of stakeholders to have direct influence on the development of an organization's culture and business operations. Literature argues in favor of organizational equity as a pre-condition for any successful

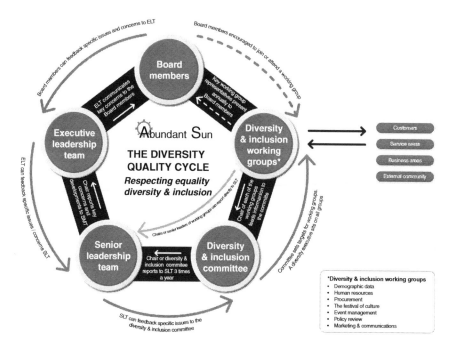

Figure 6.1 The Diversity Quality Cycle.

diversity management initiative. In addition, based on the belief organizations need effective team processes to make diversity policies and practices successful (Ely 2004), the Diversity Quality Cycle also strengthens and improves team performance, as well as the overall collective performance of a myriad of stakeholders who share common values and corporate objectives.

The Diversity Quality Cycle is built around the core value of "Celebrate and Respect Diversity." The cycle engages all key areas of an organization's core business (represented by Diversity & Inclusion Working Groups), and invites input from a variety of stakeholders (individuals and groups).

These Diversity & Inclusion Working Groups operate according to the principles of quality circles, defined as "small groups of volunteers from the same work area who meet regularly to identify, analyze and solve quality and related problems in their area of responsibility" (Munchus 1983:255; Griffin 1988:338). The vital function of working groups is to represent the views, opinions, rights, and responsibilities of each of these groups.

These working groups are designed to provide a hub of information regarding equality, diversity, and inclusion issues throughout an organization; and to generate practical and effective projects that help to improve an organization's overall diversity management performance and commitment to equality, diversity, and inclusion. These groups are informal groups, which meet to discuss and explore key issues that are having an impact upon the community. The organizational culture of each group is based on democratic processes and egalitarianism, with everyone being of equal measure and having equal influence.

It is an approach that departs from traditional diversity initiatives, featuring a central diversity committee and its associated network groups, organized around strands of equality, such as race, gender, disability, and sexual orientation. Instead of taking a traditional human resource approach to ensuring equality of opportunity and demonstrating a value of cultural diversity, the Diversity Quality Cycle, is a business-centric governance cycle which has equality, diversity, inclusion, stakeholder engagement, complexity theory, corporate social responsibility, and business ethics at its core, and which seeks to achieve more than micro-emancipations.

How the Diversity Quality Cycle works

The direction of travel

The core value of "Respecting equality diversity & inclusion" sits in the center of this diagram. The main direction of travel is clockwise, following the thick dark line from the Diversity & Inclusion Working Groups all the way around, through the Diversity & Inclusion Committee, the Senior Leadership Group, the Executive Leadership Team, and then ultimately to the members of the Board. This is the main direction of the flow of information.

Multiple stakeholders

Movement within the diagram is intended to start with the key stakeholders. In the top right-hand corner there are four rectangles, each representing a different group of stakeholders. These are: customers; service areas; business service areas; and the external community (which will include contractors, employers, partners, community groups, etc.). The vital function of these groups is to represent the views, opinions, rights, and responsibilities of each of these groups within the Diversity & Inclusion Working Groups.

Diversity & Inclusion Working Groups

There are Diversity & Inclusion Working Groups. These are represented in the bottom right-hand corner of the diagram in the rectangle. These will vary from organization to organization, and may include groups responsible for: data analytics; human resource management; policy review; procurement; events management; marketing and communications; etc.

These working groups are designed to: provide a hub of information regarding equality, diversity and inclusion issues throughout the whole organization; and generate practical and effective projects which help to improve the organization's overall performance and commitment to equality, diversity, and inclusion.

These groups, while chaired by a senior or executive leader, are informal groups that meet to discuss and explore key issues that are having an impact upon the community. There is no rank and file within these groups. Everyone is of equal measure and influence. The chair of each group then reports the progress and the outputs from their respective group to the Diversity & Inclusion Committee.

Diversity & Inclusion Committee

Being a diversity and inclusion change agent is a serious and difficult job. In selecting the other employees who will join senior executives on diversity and inclusion committees, the Diversity Quality Cycle brings an organization through a formal recruitment process. The most appropriate committee members are sought after, based on the qualities required to push the equality, diversity, and inclusion agenda. Examples of such qualities are the ability to be innovative and insightful; strong influencing skills; the ability to think strategically; a strong sense of collaboration and team working; and an ability to network.

Once the committee members are chosen, the committee then creates operational working groups, based upon its key areas of business operations. Each working group directly relates to a key business area represented in the Diversity & Inclusion Committee. To keep engagement high, those who apply for a place on the committee, but who are not chosen because they do not fulfill the selection criteria, have first choice at being members of the operational working groups.

Each working group has a member of the Diversity & Inclusion Committee within it. Through them, vital information is generated from the groups to the Diversity & Inclusion Committee. The main purpose of the committee is to: generate and analyze meaningful quantitative and qualitative data; define objectives; set targets; and monitor progress of the Diversity & Inclusion Working Groups.

There is a continual open line of communication between the Diversity & Inclusion Committee and the Working Groups. Information is fed back through the system to the various Diversity & Inclusion Working Groups and stakeholders.

The Diversity & Inclusion Committee also reports back and makes recommendations to the Executive Leadership Group three times per year.

In addition, there is also an open line of communication from the Diversity & Inclusion Working Groups through to the Senior Leadership Group (the inner thin line), by virtue of some of the Senior Leadership Team members being on the Diversity & Inclusion Working Groups. As and when key issues arise and if decisions need to be made expeditiously, there is no bureaucratic delay in raising them, as it is not necessary to wait for the next meeting of the Diversity & Inclusion Committee. In this way, the level of responsiveness is heightened and improved, and bureaucracy is diminished.

Senior Leadership Team

The Senior Leadership Team is the main group to which the Diversity & Inclusion Committee reports. It is this group that ratifies policy, makes key decisions about the allocation of resources that are presented to it by any of the Diversity & Inclusion Working Groups and the Diversity & Inclusion Committee.

When a decision needs to be made at a higher level, then those members of the Senior Leadership Team who were also members of the Executive Leadership Team are responsible for being the conduits of information to and from the Executive Leadership Team on relevant issues.

Executive Leadership Team

The Executive Leadership Team members hold all of the key business responsibilities around the issues of equality, diversity, and inclusion. The other groups that exist within the cycle are there to ensure that these responsibilities are met and exceeded in many instances. Ideally, members of the executive leadership team feed information back to their respective Board committees. For example, the Chief Financial Officer reports diversity and inclusion information to Board committees such as Finances & Resources and Remuneration. The Chief Finance Officer reports human resource and recruitment issues to a Governance & Search Committee.

Board Members

It is also through the Executive Leadership Team that members of the Board can express their views and provide guidance on how best to respond to the demands and challenges of equality, diversity, and inclusion.

Within the Diversity Quality Cycle, Board members also have the opportunity to engage directly with members of the wider organization and its community through the Diversity & Inclusion Working Groups. They may do this without interfering with the running of the business. There is an open invitation for all members of the Board to visit, discuss, and become involved with some of the activities of these groups.

This helps to close the circle, and to increase the profile of, and confidence in, the governing body. It is the intention that this will help to strengthen the overall govern-ance of the organization on the issues of equality, diversity, and inclusion.

Researchers have called for a more nuanced approach to corporate governance and diversity management that allows for high levels of stakeholder engagement, and greater equity within organizations. These conditions can leverage benefits of diversity. (Kochan et al. 2003). The Diversity Quality Cycle represents such a theoretical and practical model. It provides practitioners with information and guidance on "how" to go about effecting positive change within organizations.

7 Research for the love of action

> When it is obvious that the goals cannot be reached, do not adjust the goals, adjust the actions.
>
> —Confucius

Improving diversity and social justice outcomes requires that we address unchallenged institutional power dynamics within organizational management culture. Some contemporary diversity management researchers (Janssens and Zanoni 2005; Kersten 2000; Zanoni and Janssens 2004) believe that the avoidance of addressing management inadequacies may be instrumental in the perpetuation of inequality, discrimination, and social exclusion, resulting in ineffective diversity management and what seems to be the never-ending battle between "us and them." A similar battle spills over into the world of academic research with the main conflict existing between quantitative and qualitative researchers, their motivations and their methods. Historic power rests with quantitative scientific methodologies that attempt to prove a cause-and-effect relationship between certain variables.

A deep commitment to the reduction of social inequality through social action and community engagement spurs many people to engage in action research. Action research is defined as contributing:

> both to the practical concerns of people in an immediate problematic situation and to the goals of social science by joint collaboration within a mutually acceptable ethical framework.
>
> (Rapaport 1970:499)

The ultimate aim of action research is to facilitate changes within systems based upon the knowledge generated through past personal experience and the quantitative method. The action research framework is located within a Lewinian model. It entails:

1 identifying a general or initial idea;
2 reconnaissance mission or fact-finding;
3 planning;
4 take first step;
5 evaluate;
6 amend plan;
7 take second step.

Habermas (1971) points out that it is important to be critical about and to reflect upon the ends to be served by science. If we fail to do this then we may, intentionally or unintentionally, discover that prediction and control, which are central to quantitative methods, may prohibit understanding among and between persons and groups, as well as inhibit the release of human potential for the betterment of society.

While positivist science and action research approaches operate according to fundamentally different paradigms, intention and output, there is intrinsic value in each methodological paradigm. Problem-led quantitative research helps us to understand causal relationships. Qualitative, practice-led, action research seeks to effect social change by applying knowledge derived from quantitative methods. There is great benefit in marrying the two.

In reviewing these differences, let us compare and contrast the two approaches. Within positivist science there is neutrality of method that does not get involved with the people central to a study. Whereas, action research is designed to develop social systems that release the human potential of all of the actors.

Another main difference is that in positivist science the researcher is a detached spectator, whereas in action research, the researcher is a collaborative member of the organization being researched, and one who engages in self-reflective practice. Positivist science cannot be legitimized through the criteria of action research, and neither can action research be legitimized by meeting the criteria of positivist science.

Instead of being ensnared in the ensuing battle between researchers, perhaps the approach to take is that each approach is valuable and valid, and should be used, where appropriate. The researcher needs to have enough discernment to know when to apply which methodological approach.

Since Lewin's (1946) seminal work on action research, *Action Research and Minority Problems*, social scientists have been constantly charged by positivists to defend the relative merits of action research. The demand itself can be seen as an extension of the oppressive regime of objective scientific enquiry.

Smith (1999), in her book entitled *Decolonizing Methodologies: Research and Indigenous Peoples*, says:

> The term "research" is inextricably linked to European imperialism and colonialism ... the word itself is probably one of the dirtiest words in the indigenous world's vocabulary.

She argues that historically, science and its methods have been a Western White man's game. Personally, as an African-American female researcher, I have been taught how to play, yet I cannot accept it as the only absolute and legitimate form of research. Applying the legal constructs of anti-discrimination law to the field of scientific enquiry, I wonder if one of the consequences of the incessant demand to conform to meeting the criteria of a positivist science could itself be seen as unlawful indirect discrimination on the grounds of race, nationality, culture, and/or ethnicity. This is far too ironic.

Susman and Evered (1978) address what they consider to be a crisis in organizational science. They assert that positivistic methods lack the ability to solve real life concerns. There is a difference between knowing the potential cause of a problem, and then having the wherewithal to solve a problem and change outcomes. Positivist science may come up with the magic pill, but how does it get the patient to take it in order to change outcome?

They say:

> The crisis in organizational science is reflected in a conception of research as an accumulation of social facts that can be drawn on by practitioners when they are ready to apply them. This conception encourages a separation of theory from practice because published research is read more by producers of research than by practitioners. As a result, practitioners and their clients complain more and more frequently about the lack of relevance of published research for the problems they face and about the lack of responsiveness of researchers to meeting their needs.
>
> What appears at first to be a crisis of relevancy or usefulness of organizational science is, we feel, really a crisis of epistemology. This crisis has risen, in our judgment, because organizational researchers have taken the positivist model of science which has had great heuristic value for the physical and biological sciences and some fields of the social sciences, and have adopted it as the ultimate model of what is best for organizational science. By limiting its methods to what it claims is value-free, logical, and empirical, the positivist model of science when applied to organizations produces a knowledge that may only inadvertently serve and sometimes undermine the values of organizational members.

In comparison to positivist science, action research produces data that is highly relevant to managers and practitioners in the field. It provides them with the knowledge of what needs to be improved, and the strategies and methods to make those improvements. It is also intrinsically ethical, as the organizational members are empowered, rather than potentially exploited by the methodology. There is very little ethical risk, with the use of action research, that the "researched" will be violated and abused through the research process.

One key objective of action research is to bring about social change, and in particular, improvements in the outcomes of individual and groups who have been historically disadvantaged on several levels. Action research also sets out to empower those with whom research is conducted; it is not designed to manipulate and control individual human action, or to objectify the human existence. There are aspects of the positivistic approach that are problematic for the purposes of effecting social change.

Margaret Riel, of the Center for Collaborative Action Research,[1] states goals of action research are to:

- improve professional practice through continual learning and progressive problem-solving;
- establish a deep understanding of practice and the development of a well specified theory of action; and
- create the improvements in the community in which one's practice is embedded through participatory research.

The central objective of a diversity practitioner is to bring about greater social equity and social justice within an organizational setting. Diversity practitioners are responsible for improving the overall social performance of an organization, in order for an organization to fulfill its corporate social responsibility. Social change is at the core of any piece of work of this nature. Social change, it is argued here, is ideally brought about through collaborative processes, collective involvement, and fair processes that are designed to yield greater equity and justice within any given system.

Recently, action research has been used more widely in the field of information systems to support software implementation processes. The reason being is that:

> Project managers often lack in-depth knowledge of software implementation and development. Therefore, it is important that technology developers support project managers during such project based implementations.
>
> (Hartmann et al. 2008)

Within the field of critical management studies researchers (Eden and Huxham 1996; Spicer et al. 2009) have been utilizing action research more widely. For example, software developers have been applying the methodology of ethnography and action research in order to bring information systems from theoretical knowledge into working knowledge for the people who must use them on a daily basis. There is additional research to support the need for, and the validity of, applying ethnography and action research to the field of diversity management.

Action research and diversity management

Haseman (2006) asserts that performative researchers are "constructed as those researchers who carry out practice-led research." Practice-led research is intrinsically experiential and comes to the fore when the researcher creates new artistic forms for performance and exhibition. It is ultimately about our ability as action and performative researchers to bring creativity and innovation to our fields of research in order to change outcomes and to create new realities. It is our charge to memorize the text, to bring it to life through action, and also to use our judgment and instinct to improvise along the way.

Diversity management researchers have insisted that if progress is to be made in this area there has to be greater collaboration between researchers and practitioners. Zanoni et al. (2010) reviewed and conducted numerous studies on diversity management that span the 20 years that diversity management has been a human resource management concern. They argue that what is needed is a more performative critical diversity scholarship. They believe this can best be achieved through the use of action research. Hence, this is the main qualitative, practice-led methodology that I use in the case study presented in the next chapter.

They maintain that:

> A few diversity scholars have dared to venture into supporting real organizations in their efforts to change racial and gender relations in the workplace and have reflected on such experience.
>
> (Zanoni et al. 2010)

This is precisely what I have done in the action research case study. No one has dared me to do this; quite to the contrary, I have dared myself, as I came to imagine the consequences of my inaction to be unconscionable. Venturing into the field of action research is something that comes quite naturally to me, most likely as a result of who I am and from where I have come. Not to do so, or to be prevented from doing so, would feel both unnatural and oppressive.

Zanoni et al. (2010) plea for diversity studies which actively search for new, emancipating forms of organizing. They say:

We argue that it is time for the critical [diversity management] literature to become more performative, explicitly dealing with stimulating social change.

They speak in terms of the need for more performative critical diversity studies. Performative suggests acting, not just theorizing. Social injustice is a serious matter, and so too is the negative impact that organizations, in which power relations are abused and go unchecked, have upon the disenfranchised. Many of us have witnessed how impenetrable institutional power structures deflect and deceive, and work to correct the damage that emerges from this condition.

Micro-emancipations, arising from current models of diversity management, sublimate concerns about social justice and deceive social actors into believing they have the voice and agency to effect real, substantial, and sustainable change. We need to develop beyond the lip service, window dressing, box-ticking examples of emancipation, and aim to explore how true emancipation can be achieved through collective action. To be able to do so is a fine art.

An action research proposition

Curtis and Dreachslin (2008) suggest:

> The opportunities continue for human resource and organizational development professionals and their organizations, in collaboration with academic researchers, to build a more rigorous and extensive body of published research that directly addresses the impacts of diversity interventions.
>
> (p. 131)

The action research dimension of this book explores the extent to which diversity management can be improved through the introduction of a participative governance structure. Frustrated with the lack of progress I was seeing within organizations as an external consultant and trainer, I took a full-time, in-house position at a further education college in the United Kingdom.

As the first equality and diversity manager for this college, I had latitude to define the organization's vision and strategy. The main components of the strategy that I designed were based upon my past professional experiences of where diversity management practice needed to focus, to strengthen, and to improve. They were as follows:

- introduce diversity and inclusion framework into a predominately equality-based organization;
- build a network with high levels of stakeholder engagement through a group of voluntary supporters who could help shape and drive initiative;
- work with stakeholders to identify key areas of business in which the application of equality, diversity, and inclusion principles were essential;
- establish business-focused network groups, not demographically focused groups, which addressed business concerns;
- design a Diversity Quality Cycle, which shows governance structure as well as how information is generated and flows between different stakeholder groups within the college.

The next chapter presents an in-depth 26-month longitudinal study, tracking the organizational development of a further education institution in which the Diversity Quality Cycle, a comprehensive and innovative governance tool, is operationalized. It explores the extent to which concepts of diversity and inclusion can be integrated successfully into an organization, and whether or not this integration can yield improvements in diversity management performance.

The college provided us with a live case study, in real-life and real-time, which had great potential to enable me to determine critically whether or not strategies suggested by researchers would yield more favorable results from diversity management than traditional diversity management initiatives.

I spent 2 years and 4 months in this environment. In August 2008, I began my full-time employment as equality and diversity manager. In a re-structuring in April 2010, I was given the title of corporate responsibility development manager. I resigned by December 2010.

Note

1 Retrieved August 14, 2015 from http://cadres.pepperdine.edu/ccar/define.html.

8   An action research case study to further our education

A ship ought not be held by one anchor, nor life by a single hope.

—Epictetus

Diversity management researchers (Kochan et al. 2003) have called for an innovative and more nuanced approach to diversity management. It is believed that a new approach is required; one that allows for higher levels of stakeholder engagement, and greater equity within the workplace environment. Such conditions are thought to enable practitioners, and the organizations for which they work, to leverage the benefits of diversity better. In this action research case study, the Diversity Quality Cycle, which meets all of the above conditions, is put into practice.

This case study research explores the degree to which the activation of the Diversity Quality Cycle has the capability of improving diversity management outcomes. Thus, providing potential answers to the question of "how" to improve diversity management and make it more effective.

While traditional diversity initiatives feature a central diversity committee and equality-based network groups, such as multicultural, lesbian, gay, bisexual, and transgender, women's, and disabled network groups, the Diversity Quality Cycle departs from this. The intention of this piece of research was to break from this tradition, and to adopt a stronger business-centric governance cycle based upon equality, diversity, and inclusion, in order to improve overall diversity management effectiveness. In line with principles of complexity theory, through the process of engagement and democratic dialog between a variety of stakeholders, a pattern of governance emerged.

The Diversity Quality Cycle serves as the main framework of, and vehicle for, participatory action research. Within it, social actions take place, and data is generated, accounted, and reviewed. Strategies are adjusted in order to move closer toward the goal of improving diversity management and social justice outcomes. Central to this quality cycle are working groups that operate as Quality Circles. A Quality Circle is defined as a group of employees who perform similar duties and meet at periodic intervals, with management, to discuss work-related issues and to offer suggestions and ideas for improvements. While a mixed-method approach was used, participatory action research is the main methodology employed, within which quantitative data are generated, analyzed, and interpreted.

Why a further education college?

I sought a full-time position within an organization that would enable me to work as an in-house diversity practitioner, and to put an innovative governance structure to the test. A further education college recruited me to join its staff as its equality and diversity manager. Previously, no such role had existed within the organization. It was therefore possible to design and implement a diversity management strategy from scratch. I based my intervention on the premise that cultural change cannot be achieved by one individual alone and requires structural business mechanisms of support and multi-stakeholder engagement with intra- and extra-organizational actors (Tatli and Özbilgin 2009).

I introduced a matrix of stakeholder engagement, the Diversity Quality Cycle. What was created was a deliberative democratic practice that enabled the agency of a variety of change agents (Blackmore 2006), and the opportunity for greater management engagement with non-management staff and external stakeholders.

Background of the assignment

In August 2008, at the beginning of the research process, the organization's new corporation had been formed after two recent mergers. The first occurred in 2000, when it amalgamated three colleges in the north of the county. In January 2008, a college in the south of that county that was in special measures (i.e. had been deemed "inadequate" by the educational inspectorate) merged with the college in the north of the country. At this time, the organization agreed it would create the role of equality and diversity manager, and recruit a suitable candidate to begin the academic year of 2008/2009. This is where I stepped in.

The organization was the main provider of further education and access to higher education in its county. Its main ambition was to become a "Grade 1" college, which would mean it would be deemed "outstanding." As of September 2008, the college was a "Grade 3" college, meaning it was only "satisfactory."

Grade 1 colleges attract more funding by funding councils. There was, therefore, a strong financial dimension to the college's motivation to hire an equality and diversity manager. In order to achieve "outstanding," colleges had to demonstrate that they are high-performing institutions in the area of equality and diversity—a significant motivation for creating the role. In addition, in order to reap the financial reward, it was also necessary for colleges to demonstrate legal compliance. The organization positioned the equality and diversity manager's primary duties to be focused upon policies, procedures, student achievement data, and event management.

The two main operating principles for equality and diversity for the educational inspectorate were to close any achievement gaps between groups of students; and to tackle unfair discrimination. Consequently, senior management's priority was for the diversity management strategy to be student-centric, and not human resource management focused.

There were approximately 3,300 full-time students and 6,000 part-time students over four main campuses and seven smaller centers throughout the county. At the point of merger there were 995 members of staff in 2008/2009. In 2009/2010 there were 921 members of staff. This number reduced further in 2010/2011 after a second restructuring.

Within the county, visible ethnic diversity is low. According to the 2001 census 94.43 percent of the population was White British. This demographic was represented in the staff; however, the student population was marginally more diverse than the staff population.

In my experience of private sector organizations, diversity professionals were usually employed as part of a human resource team. This was not the case in this organization. Here, I was part of the quality improvement management team structure, and reported directly to the vice principal of quality improvements and students. I had no direct link, nor was I expected to perform any duties relevant, to human resources.

A key governance objective was to re-establish a committee responsible for setting targets and monitoring progress. The new management structure, introduced post-merger in January 2008, created a raft of executives, leaders, and managers across business. Based on past experience, and on literature on complexity theory and employee engagement, I decided the new committee should be representative of the whole business, rather than just representative of curriculum areas, as the previous committee of the dominant college in the North of the county had been. Establishing cross-organizational representation on the committee was essential in exploring how effectively equality, diversity and inclusion could be "embedded" into core business activities.

To minimize the perception that senior leaders were detached from the day-to-day realities of business, I created a governance structure in which the committee consisted only of members of the executive leadership team and the senior leadership team (i.e. the key powerbrokers). However, they did not hold sole responsibility for setting equality and diversity agendas and targets. The methodological design encourages greater stakeholder engagement and created off-shoots (i.e. working groups) of the committee. Each of these working groups had its own business focus, and was comprised of members from across the operational and strategic areas of the business. The committee members were each involved in and/or chaired a working group, and the committee was primarily responsible for monitoring progress.

Consequently, this structure created business-focused working groups that spun off the committee, each of which had a responsibility to address all of the protected characteristics outlined by current legislation (bare minimum compliance), and to operate according to the overall value of diversity and inclusion as a whole (economic imperative and moral responsibility).

The equality, diversity, and inclusion vision

The ability of the organization to achieve the vision set out was a measure of the effectiveness of diversity management strategies. Below is a 9-point comprehensive corporate vision that I constructed and presented to governors at the start of the change process in the first term of the academic year 2008/2009, to be achieved over a 3-year period:

1 Ensure an organizational culture that meets and far exceeds the bare minimum of compliance with all strands of anti-discrimination and harassment legislation (race, gender, disability, sexual orientation, religion/belief, and age).
2 Ensure a fully democratic decision-making process that understands and responds to the diversity of views and needs of all stakeholders.
3 Establish leadership that is enlightened and trusted.
4 All Board members, managers, staff, and students are highly knowledgeable about and confident to address a variety of social justice and inclusion.
5 Enhance the organization's reputation as a choice employer and as a choice service provider.

6   Dynamic products reflecting the values and standards of a global society, providing people with the skills to function effectively and ethically within diverse cultural contexts.
7   Greater cross–curricular activity, interaction, and sharing of information between groups.
8   A stronger culture of arts and entertainment that showcases and highlights a wide range of cultures and social issues.
9   Building the organization's human resource capacity to deliver on equality and diversity.

My role as equality and diversity manager was primarily to work toward the achievement of this vision.

Methodology

A mixed-method approach was used throughout this 22–month case study. The Lewinian experiential learning model was used here. The identification of the problem was the first step. The methodological approach depicted in the Lewinian Action Research Model entailed the following stages:

1   Identifying a general or initial idea: this was done as a consequence of field research and practice, having experienced first-hand shortcomings of diversity initiatives, and a general lack of structure and agreed approach to change management. Past experience within work organizations led to the research question and research methodology.
2   Reconnaissance or fact-finding: it was necessary to establish an understanding of further education as a business sector, considering its history, its key motivators around equality and diversity, and the types of alleged discrimination occurring within the sector.
3   Planning: based on knowledge of the overall corporate structure of the organization, what arose from the reconnaissance exercise was the concept of a Diversity Quality Cycle of governance within which all activities took place. Central to this cycle was the introduction of a system of governance, which was simultaneously based upon the traditional hierarchy of roles and responsibilities and based upon a system of interaction, collaboration, and communication, designed to supersede status and to enable greater equity within the change process. The main committee and business-focused working groups were created.
4   First action step: once the committee and working groups were established, the first step was to set out terms of reference of the committee and of each of its groups. These were generated by group members themselves, and informed actions of other groups. Each group decided upon key actions and objectives for the year, and devised plans that would help it achieve its goals.
5   Evaluate: evaluations had to be submitted on a regular basis throughout the year for governors, the educational inspectorate and external accountancy auditors. At the end of each academic year of research the work of the committee was reviewed. Each report served as a formal evaluation of the achievements or stumbling blocks experienced by the committee and its working groups.

6   Amend plan: based upon the outcome of the evaluations, action plans were amended and put into place in order to complete the next cycle within the next academic year. Groups reconvened and redefined terms of references where necessary and updated action plans accordingly.

7   Second step: the cycle continued with each group working collectively to achieve its aims and objectives.

Co-researchers were responsible for specifying objectives and goals; devising action plans; executing action plans; reporting on results of activity; and revising action plans where necessary in order to continue toward the achievement of specified objectives and goals.

There was further data generated from demographic data, student performance data, incident logs, and stakeholder surveys. This data is qualitative and quantitative in nature, and served to complement the qualitative data generated by action research methodological approach. This data was fed through to the committee and its relevant working groups. Actions and interventions were generated from this information.

Sampling

Approximately 100 internal stakeholders actively played parts in the Diversity Quality Cycle, which was approximately 9 percent of all members of staff, including both administrative and teaching staff. They included 13 members of the committee, all of whom were at governor, principal, vice principal, or director level (with the exception of me, the equality and diversity manager), and just under 100 internal stakeholders across eight working groups or quality circles. Additionally, external stakeholders were involved in the Procurement Working Group (i.e. contractors) and in The Festival (i.e. local council, local artists, local schools, local police, and other community groups). The number of external stakeholders fluctuated, depending upon the nature of working group's objectives and actions. All contributions made were made within the context of the Diversity Quality Cycle of governance.

In addition, a further 100 people were identified as interested in, and supportive of, the equality and diversity work of the organization. All of the above were members of a diversity mailing list that was created as a main vehicle for information exchange and dissemination. A majority of these individuals helped to organize, and/or participated in, diversity community events designed to drive the initiative forward. It was intended that all co-researchers should be self-selected, and participate voluntarily.

The working groups were created through collective involvement and discussion with a variety of stakeholders, all of whom had expressed an interest in helping to bring about positive change within the organization. An initial meeting was held on November 5, 2008 to determine what individual contributions people wished to make, that were also consistent with their professional objectives and day-to-day responsibilities to the business.

As researcher, I chaired and facilitated this collective discussion, in order to establish a clearer picture of what work needed to be done in order to improve the organization's diversity management performance. Based upon the outcome of this discussion, it was agreed that the following groups would be formed in order to provide key stakeholders with organizational conduits within which they could bring about social change: learning and teaching; marketing and communications; the learner voice (a group specifically designed to capture the views and experiences of students); procurement; festival;

staff well-being; policy review; and demographic data. These became the first seven working groups.

Data collection

The main body of research analyzed and interpreted was obtained from the following: records of historical documents of activity which took place prior to September 2008 (past learning and development); organizational inspections; past equality and diversity committee meeting minutes; minutes from committee and working group meetings which took place from September 2008 to July 2010; audits carried out by external auditing firms; and a diversity incident log which was introduced in 2009/2010. Further data was collected remotely in the form of inspection reports, up until January 2012.

There were also certain junctures at which action research yielded quantitative results through stakeholder surveys and demographic data. This data complements the main qualitative data set, and provides a measure by which progress was to be judged.

Measures

The effectiveness of a diversity management strategy was measured by the extent to which the organization could achieve its vision. Each of the working groups, and the committee, were responsible for devising and executing actions that would enable the organization to achieve its diversity management goals and realize its diversity management vision. Throughout the 22-month case study, the development of each group was tracked and measured against each group's established terms of reference, and the organization's overall vision.

Results

The following data reveals the activity of each of the eight working groups and the Diversity and Inclusivity Committee. Information contained herein, that tracked progress and barriers, is based upon the content analysis of the minutes of each working group meeting. The data enables us to assess the relative effectiveness of the diversity management strategy created through the Diversity Quality Cycle, and to identify key barriers to the organization's overall ability to improve its diversity management performance. While there was a high level of activity and productivity, there is not necessarily a positive correlation between them and improvements in diversity management and its outcomes. While some of the visions were achieved, they were short-lived and unsustainable.

Flying in the face of compliance: a case of institutional underperformance

> Vision #1: An organizational culture that meets and far exceeds the bare minimum of compliance with all strands of anti-discrimination and harassment legislation (race, gender, disability, sexual orientation, religion/belief and age).

The first and most fundamental diversity management objective to be achieved in an equality-based context was to achieve bare minimum of compliance with all strands of anti-discrimination and harassment legislation (race, gender, disability, sexual orientation, religion/belief, and age). While the organization was primarily motivated by the external demand from funding and inspectorate bodies that it be legally compliant with anti-discrimination law, this objective was not achieved fully. While there were pockets of legal compliance, some areas were left vulnerable. The main working groups responsible for addressing compliance and these vulnerabilities were: policy review; procurement; and demographic data.

The policy review team met the statutory requirement of creating a Single Equality Scheme. This document was comprehensive and produced well in advance of the date it was required. The procurement working group updated procurement policy with equality and diversity criteria.

The procurement working group was the most successful group at putting policies into practice in order to reach a higher level of legal compliance. This group ensured that all third-party organizations and contractors were aware of their legislative responsibilities and the organization's expectations of them around equality and diversity issues. The first action of this group was to revise all tendering documents to ensure the principles of equality and diversity were central criteria within account management and tender documents.

This group successfully applied these new criteria to the tender process conducted in order to identify to which company to reward a new catering contract. Key criteria addressed dietary requirements based on health (disability legislation) or lifestyle (race, religion/belief legislation). Equality and diversity were key criteria during the interview process for short-listed companies, resulting in the organization awarding the contract to a supplier who was felt to have best responded to this and other criteria.

Logging incidents

While policy compliance was achieved, there remained incidents of non-compliance within the day-to-day operations of the organization. I had been told that there had been no incidents relating to non-compliance with anti-discrimination legislation within the organizational structure pre-2008, and only three such incidents occurred throughout the academic year of 2008/2009. If this was truly the case, then there would be no need for quality improvement, and my role as equality and diversity manager would have been redundant. Feeling this highly implausible, I introduced the keeping of a formal incident log in September 2009.

During the first term of 2009/2010, from September to December, 21 incidents were captured and logged. By the close of 2009/2010, 45 incidents were brought to my attention and addressed through informal and formal procedures, in order to avoid further escalation and lodging of formal complaints. While the prevalence of equality and diversity issues within the formal complaints system remained low, through the Diversity Quality Cycle the organization was able to identify low-level concerns, and to rectify those concerns efficiently and professionally. Information contained within the incident log enabled the committee and working groups to obtain real and relevant data about areas of improvement required within the organization.

No faith in these rooms

One key area of non-compliance was identified in the provision of faith rooms across the organization's estate. Anti-discrimination legislation on the grounds of religion/

belief stipulates that this provision must be made available to all stakeholders on all organization's estates. Public corporate communication stated that it was compliant. In reality, however, only two of the four main campuses had allocated prayer rooms with signs on each door. There were no provisions at either of the seven smaller centers, which had a high proportion of English Speakers of Other Languages learners who are more likely to require such a provision for religious observation.

Rooms that had been allocated as prayer rooms had previously been used as storage rooms. Despite efforts to make the rooms more visible and accessible, and due to the lack of utilization as prayer rooms, these rooms then fell back into the default mode of being used as storage. Placing a sign on a door saying "faith room" is far from being a real indicator of legal compliance.

Closing the achievement gap

Another area of non-compliance was the organization's ability to close the achievement gap between groups of learners. The Demographic Data Working Group was responsible for overseeing this aspect of effective diversity management. Equality and Diversity Impact Measures generated from the information systems identify such gaps. In 2008/2009, post-merger, it struggled to generate accurate data that presented a clear picture of its student performance. A very informal and inaccurate system had been in place to assess the identity of students on grounds of race, gender, and disability.

According to the directors and managers who had created these statistics, they had done so by doing a headcount on who they felt fit into equality categories on which the organization had to report (i.e. race, gender, and disability). The generation of Equality and Diversity Impact Measures had not been an information systems-generated process. They were based upon individual perceptions of managers as to the social grouping of students, and were therefore extremely unreliable. Thus, there was a very strong need for a formal demographic data working group, particularly as the organization's funding and education inspectorate had become increasingly focused upon these demographic statistics and impact measures.

The organization had very limited data upon which to identity areas for improvement or to base strategic interventions. Discourse followed traditional cliché and stereotypical lines heard frequently within its sector, which were "not enough men in hairdressing" "not enough women in engineering." There was nothing more detailed or sophisticated.

The Demographic Data Working Group made great strides toward compliance, but its efforts were never fully realized. In July 2010, it put together information that informed a staff development workshop for managers, enabling them to navigate through the general information system, and to extract equality and diversity data from the system. More time was needed, but not afforded, to enable managers and their assistants to understand, interpret, and devise meaningful diversity management interventions. What was achieved was a clear understanding of where the achievements gaps were within the organization. What was not possible to achieve, however, was an effective strategy to close that gap.

Systemic and institutional limitations of information systems did not allow for further exploration of success, achievement, and/or retention rates of students based on sexual orientation, gender identity, religion, marriage/civil partnership, or pregnancy/maternity. It was therefore not possible to address the full range of groups protected under the

Equality Act 2010. By June 2010, the organization's information services had "clean" global organizational performance data, and was only then able to generate a clear picture of student achievement broken down according to age, race, gender, and disability.

An excerpt from the educational inspectorate's report of January 2012 states:

> Although the college collects data about outcomes for different groups, managers do not conduct sufficiently detailed analysis to discover whether gaps exist between the achievement of different ethnic, gender or other groups.

Democracy rules

> Vision #2: A fully democratic decision-making process that ensures the understanding of and responsiveness to the diversity of views and needs of all stakeholders.

The second part of the vision was to create a fully democratic decision-making process that ensured the understanding of and responsiveness to the diversity of views and needs of all stakeholders. This reflects the key independent variable of organizational equity, which was not a key institutional characteristic of the organization. Below are two salient examples in which democracy was tested, and won. The first relates to the choosing of the committee name; the second relates to the introduction of an induction qualification for students.

Gone to print

Toward the end of the academic year 2008/2009, I put forward a motion to the equality and diversity committee members that they might like to consider changing the committee's name, in order to reflect a more progressive approach to the inclusion agenda. The committee agreed this would be advantageous.

The process was held democratically, providing committee members with choices between the diversity and human rights committee; the diversity and inclusivity committee; and the equality and human rights committee. The majority of committee members, including the principal, voted to change the name, from the equality and diversity committee to the Diversity and Inclusivity Committee. This motion was accepted and the name was changed at the end of academic year 2008/2009. Upon this agreement, new terminology was used in printed corporate communications when they went to print, and appeared in student and staff handbooks for the coming year.

At the beginning of academic year 2009/2010, I was approached by the principal and asked to change the name of the committee back to the Equality and Diversity Committee. The rationale behind this request was that senior management wished the committee to reflect the language of the sector and external environment. The inspectorate still spoke in terms of equality and diversity. Equality and Diversity Impact Measures was the language with regards to what funding bodies were demanding as evidence of corporate performance.

When the request of senior management was put to other members of the Diversity and Inclusivity Committee, it was decided unanimously that the name could not be changed. First, the new name had been reached via democratic means. Second, this change in approach had already been committed to by virtue of the new name having gone to print in handbooks. Thus, there was no over-turning the motion; the name stood. It was already in print. The executive team had been blocked from over-turning the vote and from making a unilateral decision.

Refusing to fail

Another challenge to democracy was the introduction of a Level 2 induction qualification in equality and diversity for all students of the organization. This was the idea of an interim vice principal of curriculum who genuinely supported the agenda. However, the Learning and Teaching Working Group communicated the concerns of teaching staff who felt strongly that to introduce a qualification college-wide was both impractical and potentially detrimental to learners, teachers, and the business of the organization. With everyone being judged on success rates, the expressed fear was that many students would not pass the course examination, and that this failure would have a negative effect for individual lecturers, students, and the organization as a whole.

The use of the Diversity Quality Cycle enabled a variety of stakeholders to express and table their respective business concerns, many of which were conflicting concerns, and to find a collective solution required compromise on all parts, and which yielded the best results for all involved. Meetings and conversations resulted in senior managers agreeing upon three curriculum areas as pilot areas. They were Health and Social Care; A Levels; and Hair and Beauty. It was believed these curriculum areas were most aligned with the subject matter of equality and diversity and information would be more accessible to students. Hence students could achieve a higher level of success on the exam.

In the end, the induction qualification was offered to only one curriculum area, Health and Social Care, a curriculum area dominated by female staff and students. As anticipated, results were strong, with all 175 out of 180 students passing the exam. What was achieved was a win–win outcome, for all stakeholders, including management, though the impact was on a much smaller level than management had wished. The Learning and Teaching Working Group successfully resisted the management dictate.

Weak ethics make for weak organizations

Vision #3: An established leadership that is enlightened and trusted.

One objective was to create an enlightened and trusted leadership. What was explored was the extent to which this could be achieved by involving key leaders directly in governance processes. The hypothesis was that through mechanisms of formal (the committee) and informal governance, managers, and leaders within the organization would gain a higher degree of knowledge and understanding, and would thus be able to lead more effectively as diversity champions within the organization. While this was achieved to a respectable extent within the senior leadership team, it was not within the executive leadership team. Their knowledge and their management practice remained unchanged and discordant with the principles of diversity management.

Quantitative data that captures the general perception of stakeholders of the ethics climate within the organization, and to two salient case study examples reflect this low ethic.

There are two additional examples from working groups' accounts that also reveal a low level of leadership. The first has to do with the allocation of funds for faith rooms. Money had been generated specifically through a diversity initiative, yet the money was absorbed into and used by the wider organization, leaving the diversity function with no additional funding resource. The second is the lack of accountability and transparency with regards to an undeclared conflict of interest between an executive leader, a third-party supplier, and the organization. In October 2012, staff supported a vote of no confidence in the senior leadership team, testament to the fact that the team was perceived to have a very low level of ethical performance.

Disappearing acts

First, as mentioned earlier, the organization publicized that it was compliant in providing faith rooms on all sites, when it was not. In addition to this, the efforts of members of the staff wellbeing group to achieve compliance by renovating and redecorating designated rooms, were thwarted by the actions of an executive leader.

There was no other budget for the equality and diversity function. It was established that redecorating rooms was required in order to comply with the legislation, and that this would require some form of financial outlay. The equality and diversity function then had generated £2,000 based upon its promotion of disability equality in partnership with an organization. This money had been allocated to a special equality and diversity budgetary code to be used on general diversity initiatives. The intention was to use these funds to refurbish a variety of rooms across the campuses for general religious and health and wellbeing practices.

When it was suggested to the executive leader in charge of finance that this money be divided and spread evenly over each campus in order for the organization to comply with the legislation, the group was told that the money was no longer in the equality and diversity account. It had been absorbed into the general organization accounting system in order to make up for budgetary deficits. Therefore, despite there having been staff vision and commitment, not only were there no financial resources available to the group in order to transform rooms, there was a distinct lack of financial transparency and accountability on behalf of the organization, a position which weakened perceptions of the ethical climate within the organization.

Thus, the actions of one senior executive ran counter to the request of another senior executive. This demonstrated that their agendas were not mutually supportive. The executive leader's decision-making had a negative effect on the staff wellbeing in the working group, and members reported shock and disbelief.

Avoiding conflicts

Another key incident that reflected a lack of transparency, and consequently a low level of leadership ethics, revolved around the performance of interpreted as an organization supplying itself with agency staff, and the relationship of an executive leader to this supplier organization.

The Procurement Working Group produced a list of the Top 20 Suppliers in January 2010. This enabled members to see what percentage of the organization's revenue was being spread across suppliers. There was an agency in receipt of a majority of the organization's budgetary expenditure (approximately 15 percent). Matching this with data from the equality and diversity incidents log showed staff from this agency had engaged in a significant number of non-compliant behaviors.

A review of the corporate website of the supplier revealed it had no public expression of it valuing equality, diversity, and inclusion of its staff; no public access to diversity policies and procedures; no diversity mission statements; and no visual representation of cultural diversity on the whole of its website. This created a cause for concern. However, no dialog was established with this supplier.

In addition, it was revealed that an executive leader had a personal relationship with the owner of this agency. There appeared to be a major, though unspoken and undeclared, conflict of interest, reflecting the very low ethics climate within the organization.

It can be said that the organization was a long way from having an enlightened and trusted leadership. The work of the Diversity and Inclusivity Committee neither formed any part of executive leadership team's weekly organization-wide updates, nor did the executive leadership team genuinely engage directly or actively in the Diversity Quality Cycle of governance. The chief executive officer's addresses to the whole organization also never made mention of the core value of valuing diversity, or the work of the committee. Thus, many of the outcomes that were achieved as a result of the committee and its working groups sat in isolation from core organizational management culture.

Establishments that do not value diversity management education

> Vision #4: All Board members, leaders, managers, staff and students are highly knowledgeable about and confident to address a variety of social justice issues.

Within this case study, no staff development hours were dedicated to diversity management education. Despite the organization introducing mandatory e-learning for all staff, in order to demonstrate compliance with legislation, there were no mandatory hours dedicated to face-to-face diversity management education. This suggested that compliance was the key driver and not actual culture change.

E-learning has become an increasingly popular approach to staff development, as it saves time and money when compared to traditional forms of face-to-face staff development. While e-learning is an efficient way of delivering up-to-date knowledge and information to employees, very little empirical research has been conducted which explores the effectiveness e-learning has in substantially adding to people's knowledge and in changing people's behaviors. The exploration of personal biases, in particular, and the ability to navigate and understand a complex range of social experiences I will also argue is an exercise in real-life and in real-time. Raising personal awareness of oneself, how one has been acculturated, how one has inherited certain biases and prejudices in not learning that can be delivered most effectively by a computer program. We are talking ultimately about deep-seated belief structures that require some unpicking, and which also require the right kind of social and emotional environment to make it safe for people to do so and to be able to learn from one another.

Board members and executive leaders decided it was mandatory for staff to complete the e-learning courses on equality and diversity and safeguarding children, the two limiting grades under the educational inspectorate regime at the time. It is argued here that the main corporate function of the e-learning course was for the corporation to be able to demonstrate legislative compliance. The general climate amongst members of staff was training was part of a "box-ticking" exercise and held very little validity in terms of its ability to increase people's knowledge and to have a positive influence on behavior. Training fell into the category of "being seen to be doing something."

E-learning cannot be judged as being effective as a learning and teaching methodology (Strother 2002, Wang et al. 2007). It cannot stand alone as means of communicating knowledge, and ensuring knowledge has a positive impact upon creating more of the desired behaviors. Consequently, I tried repeatedly to gain support from governors and senior managers in making a one-day diversity awareness course, classroom-based and facilitated by me, a mandatory complement to e-learning. It was never agreed. Such support was never given and staff development in this area remained anemic.

The organization had a very professional resource at its disposal, as I had 15 years of experience delivering staff development in this area. Thus, they had access to highly professional training at no extra cost to the corporation, as it would have been delivered as part of my working responsibilities. My line manager and I had even worked this into my five key objectives for academic year 2010/2011. I would deliver a one-day Equality, Diversity and Human Rights workshop to 250 members of staff. No structural or executive leadership support, however, was ever received in order to endorse this position.

Since money was not a barrier, the remaining potential barriers to progress were time, and satisfaction that bare minimum compliance was achieved via the e-learning module. Thus, what was reinforced, intentionally or unintentionally, was the perception that the main motivation for equality and diversity activity was legal compliance. The danger of such action is that it fueled staff cynicism and disengagement, thus resulting in a counter-productive outcome for stakeholder engagement with the agenda.

Excerpt from organizational inspection in January 2012:

> However, teachers are not yet developing learners' understanding and knowledge of equality and diversity sufficiently well during lessons. The college has excellent plans to support teachers to use opportunities which arise during their lessons but, as yet, these have not been fully implemented.

This excerpt supports the findings of this research, in so much as effective diversity management strategies were developed and laid out, however, unable to be realized as a consequence of other restraints, in particular the lack of support from the Board and executive leaders.

Reputation is everything

Vision #5: Enhanced reputation as a choice employer.

From a diversity management perspective, what is considered attractive to potential and current employees is a representation of under-represented groups in the organization overall, and particularly in positions of leadership and authority. Other key attractions are family-friendly, and health and wellbeing policies. At the start of the case study the organization achieved none of these.

Workforce demographics

From an equality perspective, the organization would not qualify as being attractive to minority ethnic staff based on the statistics on racial identity. Of the country's population, 94.43 percent was White British. The White British staff population was 90.85 percent.

There were several ethnic groupings in which staff members were below the population percentage according to demographic data obtained from the 2007 census.

For 2007/08 the staff demographics were:

- Mixed: White and Black Caribbean (County, 0.29 percent; Staff, 0.13 percent).
- Mixed: Other Mixed (County, 0.22 percent; Staff, 0.19 percent).
- Asian or Asian British: Other Asian (County, 0.16 percent; Staff, 0.13 percent).
- Black or Black British: Other Black (County, 0.04 percent, Staff, 0 percent).
- Chinese or Other Ethnic Group: Chinese (County, 0.31 percent; Staff, 0.06 percent).

There were no formal strategies put in place to change workforce demographics, and these figures did not improve throughout the 22 months of the case study. To the contrary, particularly in the management category, the numbers worsened with the departure of a female director and me.

The disability and sexual orientation data was also discouraging. There were concerns about mental health and sexual orientation issues. The incident log flagged several instances of mismanagement of staff members with mental illness and homophobic behavior amongst staff and students, sometimes resulting in alleged bullying.

The organization had a very low percentage of members of staff (1.8 percent) who had declared disabilities. This number is significantly disproportionate to the number of citizens throughout the county who are disabled and of employment age (13.41 percent), and of the number of learners within the organization (13.18 percent) who were disabled. This suggested there was enormous scope for increasing the number of disabled staff within the organization, as the current figure is not representative of other populations. There was no data generated to reflect sexual orientation, as a conscious managerial decision was made that the organization was "not ready" to monitor it.

The organization benefited from its position of being the largest and only provider of further education and access to higher education courses in a county. Consequently, the organization wielded a high-level employer power as a consequence of this monopoly. The staff wellbeing group was created in an attempt to counterbalance this position, and to improve diversity management performance within the context of human resource management. This group was the least successful of all of the working groups, reflecting the sector's overall tendency to overlook the needs of staff in favor of the performance outcomes for customers.

Staff wellbeing

The main short-term objective of the staff wellbeing group was to re-draft the previous Healthy Lifestyle policy that had been created by a member of the human resource team. The task proved to be very difficult and no consensus was reached as to what the policy should contain. There were concerns about the inflammatory potential of introducing such a document, and the effect this might have on the overall culture and morale of staff. The assumption was that this policy move may have had a negative impact.

In the summer term of 2010, it was decided it would be beneficial for the working group to hold staff focus groups on each of the main campuses, in order to engage staff in the process of policy creation. As the corporation was undergoing its second restructuring and redundancy exercise in two years, the climate was very tense and the position of human resources was compromised. A majority of staff members felt vulnerable as a consequence of being labeled as "at risk," and did not wish to be seen as trouble-makers. The policy was never completed, and never saw its way to the policy review team. A draft was neither put out to staff nor the unions for consultation. Staff morale continued to weaken, which may have resulted in the vote of no confidence in the senior management team in October 2012.

The struggle to improve the curriculum

> Vision #6: A dynamic curriculum reflecting the values and standards of a global society, providing our learners with the skills to function effectively and ethically within diverse cultural contexts.

This had been the objective of the Learning and Teaching Working Group. Continual attempts were made to interface with various curriculum areas in order to inform them of best diversity and inclusion practice. However, many of these attempts were insufficient. Despite all efforts made to improve diversity management, it had not been achieved by the end of the case study. Efforts were deemed insufficient in their ability to achieve legal compliance or to create the level of culture change required. An Internal Quality Audit of the curriculum was carried out by an external body in the autumn term of 2010 which highlighted the organization's cultural inadequacies.

The report highlighted "insufficient promotion of equality and diversity, every child matters, and safeguarding in lesson planning and delivery in essential skills" and an "insufficient reinforcement of learner safeguarding and equality and diversity in classrooms and throughout the organization." It also suggested that the organization needed to "improve aspects of the provision for equality and diversity, for example the establishment of equality and diversity impact measures and equality impact assessments and the use of data in self-assessment to support equality and diversity."

The report also reflects the fact that there was still a great deal of work to be done by the Demographic Data Working Group to improve impact measures and to actually have a positive effect on closing the achievement gaps between groups. It notes that the Policy Review Working Group was at the very start of its journey to having a clear and effective system in place in order to assess objectively and fairly the impact that organizational policies had on key stakeholders, and in ensuring that this impact was not against anti-discrimination law.

Rigid identities: the challenge of breaking down silos

> Vision #7: Greater cross-curricular activity, interaction and sharing of information between our learner groups.

The annual event to celebrate diversity across the organization was an attempt to overcome a siloed institutional culture. The dominant age group was full-time 16–18 students, the group from which the organization obtained most of its funding. There was very little participation from other curriculum areas or age groups.

In terms of age, the largest student population was those between the ages of 17–18 (34.07 percent). They would have attended as a consequence of their tutors booking their classes on to the event. The second largest population was those within the 35–50 range (23.08 percent); this group most likely constituted staff and external community contributors.

Out of five directorates—Service Industries; Creative Industries, Business and Management; Technology, Science and the Built Environment; Foundation Skills; and Land Based and Leisure Industries—the highest level of activity was within two: Service Industries (Health and Social Care; Catering and Hospitality; and Hair and Beauty); and Foundation Skills (Essential Skills; and English Speakers of Other Languages). Creative Industries was involved primarily from a broadcasting point of view.

These two directorates combined represent a very high proportion of females, and a majority of the organization's disabled learners and its non-United Kingdom nationals. The festival was seen primarily as something for those individuals and groups who were underrepresented in the category of race and disability. Thus, a high proportion of under-represented groups were participating. It appeared to be a minority-driven event, and lacked the essence of diversity and inclusion. There was, therefore a very strong equality focus to the culture, as the event struggled to increase in diversity and to be inclusive of all stakeholders within the organizational culture.

Driving culture change through creativity and innovation

> Vision #8: A stronger culture of arts and entertainment that showcases and highlights a wide range of cultures and social issues.

To bring the Single Equality Scheme to the attention of stakeholders, a public event was designed and held at one of the organization's main sites. The event, which took place in January 2010, consisted of the screening of a new BBC period film for television that was aired in December 2009, and which dealt dramatically with issues of race, disability, and other diversity issues. The organization invited one of the film producers to take part in a post-film discussion. This special screening event attracted 135 stakeholders from across the community, including representatives of students, staff, catering contractors, community groups, statutory partners, and friends and family.

An event questionnaire was distributed to 130 attendees. Fifty-eight responses were received. Using a 4-point scale, with 4 being excellent and 1 being poor, participants were asked to rate the organization's commitment to equality and diversity and also its success at achieving equality. Organizational commitment scored 3.25; organizational success scored 3.18.

General comments received about the event:

Program
"It opened my mind to racism and how bad it really was and still is."
"More please!"
"Excellent to have the discussion after."
"Resonates with my life in the southwest. Brilliant."

Benefit
"Great to see such a mix of people in the room."
"Shows what Jamaicans had to go through and, no matter what, they still wanted to live in Britain and still go through racism of prejudiced people."
"With delivery in course program."
"Helps with understanding of college course work."
"Very beneficial to make a greater understanding of college course unit work."
"Supports diversity unit."

"It showed me a big insight into Black and White cultures."
"It opened my eyes to so many equality issues."
"Yes. Uplifting."

Data suggests that the use of film and media as a tool for education and community development was effective. Through a collective effort, driven by the Diversity Quality Cycle, this event engaged a wide variety of stakeholders in an entertaining and highly educational learning event, which addressed many forms of historical discrimination and prejudice. The level of employee and community engagement in the event was extremely high in terms of attendance at the event, and post-screening discussion about issues raised by the film.

All who attended the event were part of the action research process, and contributed collectively to sharing knowledge, experience, and information that resulted in a substantial increase of equality, diversity and inclusion awareness, and to the strengthening of the multicultural environment within which people are living and working. It was deemed to be a great success and was heralded by many, including governors and the senior management team.

Educational DVD production

As part of managing the organization's external community relations, the health and safety manager became involved in a government agenda to identify individuals vulnerable to radicalization by terrorist groups. Members of the group represented the organization, the county council, the police, the fire service, local schools, and local community groups. The aim of the group was to assist in the delivery of the government's agenda to improve community cohesion and to reduce the development of extreme terrorism.

The organization proposed to undertake the making of a DVD and creation of a website that highlighted experiences of Muslim people living in the county, with a view of integrating learning material into the curricula of the college, other educational institutions, and organizations. A proposal was put forward to the local council to complete the project via the college's media arts department, with guidance from the innovations manager. A budget of £4,000 was granted to the college by the council for completion of the project. While the project was not completed by the end of the study, it was successfully completed in September 2011.

Very strong community relations were established with partner organizations throughout this time. A community of mutual support developed, and was built upon by members involved. An excellent learning tool was produced, but due to my departure from the college and the departure of my counterpart in the local council, no one took ownership of the product in order to ensure the impact was extensive and sustainable.

Put your money where your mouth is

Vision #9: Building the organization's capacity to deliver on equality and diversity.

Overall, the voice and agency of the diversity champions within the organization was very low. In addition, another thing that was distinctly missing was financial power, and human resource to support positive diversity management developments.

Financial investment in the diversity management function was very low, and, as noted earlier in reference to the reallocation of funds, was even at times removed. This made it difficult to progress, and harder to meet the objectives of improving the effectiveness of diversity management.

In the first year of the case study, a budget of £5,000 was allocated to the diversity function by the organization specifically for the design and delivery of the college's annual celebratory event in the first year. These funds, however, were not sufficient to ensure the delivery of an inclusive event. Through partnership with the local council, I was able to secure an additional £3,000 in sponsorship from the local council. This brought the budget up to £8,000 for the May 2009 event. It was successfully delivered, and on a scale larger than the inaugural event which had taken place in May 2008.

By the May 2010 event, the organization had not allocated an operating budget for the equality and diversity function at all. The function was wholly reliant upon the sharing of financial contributions from other areas of the college that had funds in their local budgets.

During this time of financial retraction, my influence and authority was revoked from the management team. In September 2008, when initially hired, I was part of the senior leadership team, which was chaired by my line manager. Upon his redundancy the chair was taken over by the executive leader in charge of resources, including finance. It was he who, rather than give us greater seniority in line with our colleagues, made the decision to remove the staff development manager and the equality and diversity manager from the group.

From a staffing point of view, rather than increasing the number of staff working on diversity, the role of equality and diversity manager was removed from the corporate structure. When I resigned from my managerial role in December 2010, the college did not advertise for a replacement. One year later a new hire was appointed; an equality and diversity officer within a post that had been downgraded in seniority and pay.

The Diversity Quality Cycle was disbanded in January 2011. The only thing that remained as part of the public marketing and communication was the Single Equality Scheme and the cultural celebratory event. Eventually, these too would disappear from the landscape.

In May 2011, the event for which the equality and diversity manager had been responsible was now the responsibility of a junior member of staff, with no working group to support her. The event took the form of an equality and diversity questionnaire emailed to staff, requesting that it be shared with students. The level of engagement and stakeholder participation had dropped significantly, as had the impact of the "event" on the wider organizational culture, and its ability to meet its equality and diversity objectives.

In September 2011, the organization downgraded the post of equality and diversity manager to equality and diversity officer, and advertised the post. There was a reduction in managerial power as well as salary. An appointment was made in December 2011, one year after my departure. By this time, the educational inspectorate had removed equality and diversity as a limiting grade in inspection. The importance of legal compliance, in order to attract funding, had diminished profoundly. The priority was even weaker than it was before. Voice and agency of the diversity professional and the other diversity champions within the organization had been reduced substantially.

In January 2012, the organization underwent a full inspection. In its previous 2007 inspection, it had received a "3" meaning satisfactory. In 2012 it yielded exactly the same result, showing no movement at all in terms of quality improvement, despite

4 years of organizational development efforts to raise the college to a Grade 1 college. This ambition continued to elude the organization.

Leadership and management was given a "3" meaning satisfactory. Equality and diversity performance was also given a "3" meaning satisfactory, which showed a deterioration from the "2" meaning good it had received in a partial inspection in 2009/2010.

The 2012 report says:

> Equality of opportunity is satisfactory and the college has a culture of mutual respect between all participants. Analysis of equalities data is insufficient to enable the college to be fully confident that there are no gaps in the achievement of different groups of learners. Strategies to help teachers develop learners' wider knowledge of diversity during lessons are not well established.

What does the college need to do to improve?

> Ensure that equality and diversity are promoted effectively in lessons by providing effective staff development and ensuring that teaching observations consistently report on the quality of this work in lessons.
>
> However, strategies to help teachers develop learners' understanding and knowledge of equality and diversity during teaching sessions, and how these would apply to their work in areas such as customer service, are not as yet well established.

How far this embedding went may be directly related to the external demands of corporate accountability; the quality of the corporate motivation of governors and senior management; the management quality of the corporate culture; the availability of financial resources; the quality of diversity education; and time dedicated to dialog.

Discussion

By the time of my resignation in December 2010, it can be argued that some of the 3-year vision created in 2008 had been achieved, but that this performance had not been embedded in the institution. Not only was performance unsustainable, in some instances it was either negated, or going backward. While there was a significant amount of stakeholder goodwill and a substantial level of organized stakeholder engagement, there was no demonstrable positive change reflecting increases in diversity management performance and outcomes.

Nonetheless, the Diversity Quality Cycle provided a mechanism of inclusive and participatory governance that allowed for the embedding of equality, diversity, and inclusion throughout an organizational culture. It provided a framework that addressed traditionally marginalized groups, as well as a framework that enabled new forms of knowledge and conversations about inequity that went beyond traditional understanding and rhetoric.

The operating model of the Diversity Quality Cycle enabled the organization to address key equality and diversity business concerns, and to improve its equality and diversity performance, through the Cycle's system of structured and participative governance. It enabled stakeholders to address traditional equality concerns such as race, gender, and disability, as defined by anti–discrimination legislation. And it highlighted more subtle forms of diversity and inequalities existing within the organization that stretch beyond legislation.

All working groups functioned as quality circles, primarily for staff, but with the inclusion of other stakeholders such as students and community groups. What is most important is that no working group was self-contained. The Diversity Quality Cycle allowed for cross-fertilization between groups, and for each group to support the work of other groups where possible, thus building the cohesive fiber and strength of initiative.

The Quality Circles (i.e. working groups) provided space for dialog and critical thinking; they provided a key mechanism for staff development and continued professional development. The learning that took place as a consequence of dialog and exchange provided a high level of legal education, awareness building, and business development skills to those who participated within the Quality Circles.

The Diversity Quality Cycle provided more time and space for reflection and learning. I believe that such active participation is far more effective than the way in which traditional diversity committees function. The Diversity Quality Cycle provided a much more business-focused and cost-effective approach to embedding equality, diversity, and inclusion into core business, and in informing stakeholders of their main roles and responsibilities.

Another example of the effectiveness of the Diversity Quality Cycle was that it provided a mechanism to embed a variety of corporate values, not just a "respect and celebrate diversity" into organizational culture. As working groups presented themselves, and engaged in their agendas functioning as Quality Circles, it became apparent each group had a contribution to make to at least one of the other core values. Therefore, this was not just a diversity management initiative. It was a corporate initiative that provided structural mechanisms for key business areas to strengthen performance around a variety of core corporate values. For instance, core value #4 was to "empower staff to maximize their potential"; this was supported by the staff well-being group. Core value #2 was to "deliver outstanding quality and innovation"; this was achieved by the Diversity, Learning and Teaching quality circle.

Participation in working groups provided all co-researchers with an opportunity to deepen their understanding about equality and diversity, and to deepen their understanding of how principles must be applied to their specific business areas as well as to the college's overall business environment. This on-the-job training took place for each individual at least once a quarter. It is argued here that the quality of such engagement, and the practical outcomes which arose out of this engagement, far outweighed the benefits of any results seen from diversity awareness training, which is limited to e-learning or classroom learning.

In spite of the Diversity Quality Cycle's effectiveness, other organizational barriers were in place that may have contributed to the blocking of further progress. One key barrier was that none of the other key groups within the Diversity Quality Cycle (i.e. the Senior Leadership Group, the Executive Leadership Group, or the Board of Directors) was organized along these lines. These groups continued to be ordered around a traditional command and control style of governance, or managerial capitalism. In addition, members of leadership groups that did not participate in Diversity Quality Cycle dialogs did not reap the same benefits of education and awareness obtained by those who were directly involved in the Diversity Quality Cycle.

Organizational regimes of inequality starve diversity managers of strategic resources, and restrict their capacity to take action (Tatli and Özbilgin 2009). Traditional rigid structures reinforced institutional inequities, thus making it difficult for working groups to be fully effective, and for the overall exercise to been seen as more than a box-ticking exercise. Delegating responsibility through traditional "command and control" management may be a profoundly limiting factor in the lack of diversity management's sustainability in the long-term development of an organization.

Despite collective efforts put into the agenda by a large number of co-researchers, the resultant belief was that the overall exercise was still merely a "tick-box" exercise. De-moralization and cynicism developed in light of such circumstances, reminding us that diversity initiatives can at times do more harm than good, particularly if initiatives raise expectations that cannot be met due to institutional resistance.

I assert that the quality and knowledge of leadership plays a very large role in an organization's ability to "embed diversity" into its business culture and to improve its social performance, thus sustaining any gains achieved throughout the process. Each working group made demonstrable progress in each of their business areas. The equitable exchanges that highlighted many key issues, and generated many constructive and creative interventions were contained. As a result of the wider organizational culture continuing to operate on a "command and control" model of management, information generated, and suggestions made for more challenging improvements (i.e. mandatory face-to-face diversity awareness staff development), were neither taken up, nor acted upon, by the Board members, executives, or senior leaders.

The question of the sustainability of the diversity management strategy must be set against the backdrop of ethical and sustainable executive and senior leadership, of which there was none in this case study. From this has arisen the realization of just how important the 3Es—ethical, engaged, and enlightened—of leadership are. While many of these qualities were exhibited at director level in the case study organization, most of these qualities were distinctly absent in the senior management team as a whole. This was a major block to organizational development and to the success of the diversity management strategy.

With such organizational and leadership instability, it is highly unlikely that any diversity management strategy could survive the test of time, if leaders themselves do not survive, or if they lack the knowledge and ethics to carry a diversity management campaign. Work carried out within the college appears to support concerns that diversity falls off the radar screen as committed leadership declines, and as the importance of it, from a compliance and risk management point of view, diminishes in light of external conditions (i.e. financial crises and reduction of regulatory pressure).

The results of this study highlight: the instability of senior management and college leadership group teams; economic strain; the institutionalized nature of hierarchical, non-collaborative, top-down management running counter to the principles of equality of opportunity and the valuing of diversity; rapidly changing regulatory environments; apathy of staff due to lack of knowledge and/or low morale; perceptions of risk of non-compliance to anti-discrimination legislation; regular corporate restructuring; cultural and historic divisions between campuses, staff, and curriculum areas; and entrenched curriculum areas making it difficult to effect wide-scale and sustainable change.

It appears possible, that using the Diversity Quality Cycle has the power to embed equality, diversity and inclusion into core business functions, but not without the 3Es — ethical, engaged, and enlightened—of leadership behind it. With this lack of good, strong, enlightened leadership, it can be argued that the existence of the committee, its working groups and the equality and diversity manager were primarily to appease stakeholders, funding bodies and inspectorates.

What was achieved through the Diversity Quality Cycle were micro-emancipations. It can certainly be argued that, as a consequence of the fundamental rigidity of the management culture, alongside its motivations, lack of engagement, poor leadership ethic and low priority of diversity management, diversity management activities were self-contained and could neither influence the wider organizational culture, nor achieve long-term positive outcomes.

Limitations

The case study lasted for 22 months. During this period, qualitative and quantitative data was generated that shed light on key issues of concern for the corporation and its stakeholders. Some of the data was retrospective (i.e. demographic data) and provided information about past conditions. In order to improve the overall quality of equality and diversity performance, key actions and interventions were suggested. The study neither provided enough time, nor consistent organizational structure to follow through on these recommendations. It was not possible to see and realize the potential for change.

The sustainability of change has yet to be demonstrated. With the focus upon long-term growth and sustainability, the short-term nature of this study does not provide us with enough information in order to ascertain whether or not the diversity management strategy and the initiatives devised within the context of the Diversity Quality Cycle have the capability of yielding long-term and sustainable growth and improvements in business performance overall. I do believe that if the diversity and inclusion work had really had the support of the senior leadership team then the initiative would have survived and thrived, and long-term sustainable improvements would have been made. The lack of ethical and committed leadership within the institution was very much the demise of effective diversity management.

Key emergent themes and potential barriers to effective diversity management

The participatory action research project, and particularly work carried out within the Diversity Quality Cycle, revealed and captured several factors which may contribute to ineffectiveness of diversity management strategies. It can be argued that one key barrier to progress was low staff retention. This is particularly salient among the college leadership group, the management group responsible for key governance of equality, diversity, and inclusion agenda.

In 2009/2010 the college had to find savings of £1.5 million. This resulted in another round of restructuring and redundancy. During the academic year 2010/2011 the college was faced with a further £3 million budget cut, and underwent another round of restructuring and redundancies, this time losing approximately 86 more staff. The staff passed a vote of no confidence in the senior management team. Out of the four senior managers hired to run the organization in 2008, none remained by 2013.

At the beginning of 2008/2009 there were 25 members of the college leadership group, 13 of whom formed the Diversity and Inclusivity Committee. By the end of the study, of the original 25 members, only 11 remained. Fifty-six percent of the top leadership tier was not retained. This included three out of four original executive leaders, six senior leaders and two managers. Six of the senior leadership group members, each of whom had been a chair of one of the working groups, left during this 2-year period. There was one original chair remaining when the case study ended.

Economic volatility and uncertainty had a serious impact upon the diversity management strategy within the college, particularly upon the staff wellbeing group. This cannot be over-looked when evaluating the ability of the team to meet key objectives, and for the overall objective of the diversity management initiative.

In general, what was highlighted in the action research was:

- controlling/hierarchical corporate culture;
- low value given to and priority placed upon human resources;
- no structured and dedicated time for learning and development for any group of stakeholders;
- face-to-face diversity educational hours were not taken by staff;
- executive leaders disengaged with and separate from other stakeholders;
- the predominance of a compliance-driven agenda and language;
- culture entrenched in three traditional equality strands: race, disability, and gender. Gender equality was written into policy documents; however there was no real discussion or action taken to ensure gender equality;
- attempts to introduce the language and concepts of inclusion and human rights were partially successful, yet unsuccessful in informing the manner in which the wider organization was governed;
- diversity activities very limited strategically as they revolved primarily around corporate communications and external relationships. Nothing was established with regards to: diversity training; professional development; recruitment; infrastructure; and retention;
- staff retention was poor. Staff redundancy and turnover rate too high to sustain the diversity management strategy;
- very low organizational equity;
- poor retention rate of employees.

It can be argued that, as a consequence of the existence of these barriers, the diversity management strategy functioned primarily as a public relations campaign, and little internal change took place within the college over the 22-month period of research.

It may be that a combination of the variables above had an impact on the effectiveness of diversity management strategy. As noted in the literature review of this book, one aspect of diversity management practice that has been critiqued most is diversity training. It is argued that if diversity training is in place within an organization, it cannot exist in isolation from the other variables listed above. There are specific organizational conditions, conditions that reflect organizational equity and stakeholder engagement that are most likely to contribute to the effectiveness of a diversity management strategy.

Recommendations for future research

Collaboration between researchers and practitioners should continue, in the form of longitudinal projects undertaken and carried out for a minimum of 5 years, in order to track progress and establish diversity management effectiveness and improvements that can be made to the Diversity Quality Cycle. It presents a more complex and nuanced approach to diversity management, and clearly defines the amount of time, energy and resource required in order to improve social performance of an organization.

Future research could explore the impact that introducing the Diversity Quality Cycle has on organizations which have operationalized a traditional approach to diversity (i.e. management through the introduction of committees, and social network groups organized around individuals protected characteristics (i.e. race, gender, sexual orientation, age) and organizations that have had no prior diversity initiatives in place. Research can be done to establish whether or not diversity performance is accelerated, remains the same, or is slowed down by introducing the Diversity Quality Cycle as a governance tool.

The diversity working groups formed part of the Diversity Quality Cycle, organized around the principles of quality circles. Short-term results were achieved; long-term sustainable change was not. Future research could focus upon creating Quality Circles within senior management groups within an organization. This can either be done within the formal management meetings, or researchers can experiment with changing ways in which "formal" meetings are run and managed. Research can focus upon whether or not democratic dialog, long-term solutions, and organizational changes can be sustained by engaging senior managers and Board members in Quality Circle dialogs.

Attention must be paid to continually challenging financial and legal environments, and the strain this change places upon the social performance of organizations. Future research can explore the extent to which a company can improve its social and ethical performance if it does not abort the Diversity Quality Cycle in times of uncertainty and crises, and instead uses the Diversity Quality Cycle to help it identify collective solutions to collective problems shared by all stakeholders.

Such an approach may enable senior decision-makers to: address, rather than avoid, discussions of the high levels of uncertainty with which they are faced; engage rather than control; and find fairer and more democratic solutions to problems that their businesses are facing today. While our global economic model is under serious question, now is the time to build new models of management, and new approaches to capital, that will allow for growth and expansion, and provide an exit route into the future.

9 Confessions of a diversity and inclusion practitioner

> I shall never be a heretic; I may err in dispute, but I do not wish to decide anything finally; on the other hand, I am not bound by the opinions of men.
>
> —Martin Luther

The main objective of this book is to explore how to make diversity management strategies more effective, with regards to social justice performance outcomes. It is also to explore how we could become better diversity practitioners, researchers, and leaders, or perhaps even how and why we should be them at all.

The objective of the action research process is to improve upon practice, understanding of practice and conditions within which practice takes place (Carr and Kemmis 1986). This sits primarily within the category of the agency of diversity managers. Did my practice improve? What did I learn? How have I become a better practitioner? What has this process confirmed for me? Where did I begin? Where did I end?

Experience had taught me an inclusive definition of diversity, one that is based upon respect for the individual, regardless of social categorization. My a priori belief, going into the action research process, was that individuals and groups of students and workers would be experiencing unfair treatment, or discrimination, that may or may not reflect the traditional discourse around equality and diversity.

Key practical insights

Beyond "We must be seen to be doing something"

"We must be seen to be doing something" is a phrase that I have heard many times within the context of government responses to external pressures. In my experience it merely suggests we have to show some form of token action in order to protect reputation and standing. It is window-dressing. The quality and relevance of this action often seems to be of little importance.

My existence within the host system was a direct response to external pressure from funding bodies in particular, and motivated by a need to protect revenue streams at a time when economic recession was threatening to recede further. That is how it began. Circumstances for colleges intensified in September 2009 when Ofsted made equality and diversity a limiting inspection grade. If colleges could not demonstrate, not only a value for equality and diversity, but also the reality of proactive commitment being expressed in real demonstrable changes in social justice and social equity, then a college's grade could not reach "outstanding." Funding is directly proportional to inspection grades; the higher the grade, the more money a college receives. Thus, the push was on. I wound up feeling as though I was a "trophy" employee, a status symbol for the corporation, nothing more, and nothing less.

I was hoping that my actions, and those of others, would free the college from this cycle of reputation management and bare minimum legal compliance. Based on the experience and knowledge I was bringing to the role, I was hopeful I would be able to bring these talents to bear and effect significant and substantial improvements in social justice. This was not my experience. The experience was overall disempowering.

In the beginning

I was enthusiastic about the potential for change, and the positive impact I could make bringing my experience, particularly my private sector experience, to a rural organization where there was not traditionally defined cultural diversity. I was looking forward to being part of a team, and the architect and main director of a medium-term strategy.

In beginning, I was part of the senior leadership and the quality management teams, and looked forward to having a leadership influence on the college. While the composition of these two groups was primarily individuals at senior management and director level, two managers were included: the staff development manager and me, the equality and diversity manager. I was happy with my title as manager, as long as I felt there was scope for influencing, developing, and directing performance. I did hope it was a matter of time before my title became consonant with my actions. I possessed a lot of patience, as my role was new for the organization.

The deficit model—speaking a foreign language

A culture shock was the extent to which organizational language was reflective of a very old-school equalities agenda, one that the private sector had long since evolved beyond, but had not left completely. I found myself living within a deficit model, where people spoke about minorities needing help and assistance, be it counseling or learning support. There was no real discussion of the benefits that come with diversity. This presented a struggle, as it was clear to me I had to challenge the status quo in terms of awareness, even of those who had been champions of the equality agenda prior to my arrival.

The reign of terror

The senior leaders team members expressed a continual "threat" of Ofsted and fear of inspection. Fear, trepidation, anxiety, and panic appeared to become the common organizational ethos. With it came a heightened "we need to be seen to be doing something," in order to safeguard reputation and reduce jeopardizing future funding streams. This falls into the reactionary pattern of the equality framework.

Senior leaders placed high levels of pressure upon staff to perform, yet did not provide them with adequate knowledge or tools to do able to do so satisfactorily, let alone outstandingly. With this dominant top–down capitalistic managerial approach, which imposes without consulting, a climate of suspicion and cynicism about the intentions of management ran high. Such a dictatorial approach in itself can be seen to be socially unjust, and has great capacity to be counter-productive in encouraging people to value and respect equality and diversity; it is certainly not inclusive. It can leave workers asking the question "If I am not cared for, then why should I care for others?" The diversity and ethics climates were very low.

My personal approach as equality and diversity manager was not to fall into what I considered to be a trap. I felt it was necessary to exude confidence and caring about all stakeholders and ensured this was a part of my communication with my colleagues. I was confident I knew what "outstanding" looked like from an equality, diversity, and inclusion point of view, and continued building the project with the help of my colleagues. Working groups members by and large reflected: a real sense of commitment to the social justice agenda; a desire to look at the organizational system critically; and a real desire to see performance improve.

Equality of opportunity had been graded as "good" in the organization's 2007 inspection; that was without the structures put in place from 2008–2010. Despite the grading becoming more stringent under the new inspection regime of 2009, provided we were able to build upon work prior to the merger in January 2008, I had confidence we could maintain "good." Without shifts in the level and quality of senior leadership participation, and in the absence of a value for human resources, I saw the possibility of rising to "outstanding" in equality of opportunity as a very long game.

By the end of academic year 2008/2009, the data led me to believe something must be done proactively to invest in and support staff, as so much of the success of diversity management was predicated on staff performance. The eighth and last working group to be added to the Diversity Quality Cycle was the Diversity and Staff Wellbeing Group. It was introduced in September 2009. No headway was made toward having a positive impact upon top-down management, or on the fundamental approach to governance (i.e. new public management and capitalistic managerialism) within the organization. This, coupled with a high turnover of members of the executive and senior leadership teams, made diversity management efforts discontinuous and unsustainable.

Clash of the titans

The first key priority was to re-establish the equality and diversity committee. Prior to the merger, there was a committee in the North of the county, which consisted primarily of leaders and managers. There was also a committee in the South of the county. The South's equality and diversity committee consisted of a wide range of employee representing a cross-section of functions across the organization.

Knowing how important collective involvement and collective action is in driving social change, I knew I wanted to have a broad range of people involved in the social change process. The first meeting of those interested in participating was held in November 2008, with a total of approximately 30 people. It clearly was not possible to have a committee with over 30 members. I was therefore tasked with grouping people according to personal passions/commitments that matched with their professional skills and responsibilities. I had to ensure I did not alienate anyone by excluding them from the governance process. It occurred to me what might be effective was to create working groups reflective of key business concerns, and to have these working groups function as mechanisms by which the objectives of equality and diversity committee would be achieved.

It also occurred to me that the committee alone should not set objectives but that working groups, as they are closer to the ground of business operations, should also be instrumental in defining and directing activity. It was therefore, going to take some time to re-construct the equality and diversity committee and to get it into a form in which it was a fully functioning part of the organization's wider governance system.

When called upon by the members of the Board to present a progress report, they had been given minutes of the November meeting, and were startled by the number of people in attendance. They assumed these people were all committee members and highly criticized me for the sheer number of people, saying it was more like an "audience" than a committee. They expected the committee to have already been formed. I was not given time to explain the process by which committee and its working groups were being co-created by those involved. I left the meeting feeling bullied and demoralized, yet determined to make the governance structure work.

I was spoken to in what I considered a very aggressive, humiliating, and condescending manner. I fundamentally understood there was a desire to "get equality and diversity right," and the way in which I had been treated may not have been a reflection of the intention or true character of those who put me in the line of fire. It appeared as though they had not developed the capacity to listen to that which they were not expecting to hear. I realized I felt responsible for finding a way to engage governors in a process of learning about equality, diversity, and inclusion in order to reduce hostility and misunderstanding.

Beyond mediocre targets

In my first year, I had five key professional objectives I had to meet. As a creative person, and social entrepreneur, I was accustomed to working independently; I was not accustomed to sticking rigidly to pre-determined objectives. I met my five objectives and many more, as I did not feel bound by them, and had the drive and determination to do much more than what was expected. So, of my own volition, my equality and diversity work had greater span than what was desired by the corporation.

In addition, in the beginning, I was happy to go "above and beyond the call of duty." One of the ways in which I demonstrated my commitment and my team spirit was by taking on responsibility for an A-Level Psychology class. This added enormous pressure to my weekly schedule, as I had to prepare for and deliver a 3-hour class weekly. For me it was a labor of love, which I had falsely assumed would be demonstrably appreciated by the organization. It never was. Not only was no additional contract drawn up for this role I fulfilled, I was not even financially remunerated for my time and effort. At this point, I had to call into question the ethics of the wider governance of the organization (the ethical climate). I knew from then I had to be self-protective (defensive) rather than collaborative.

I discovered I would go into what I coined "energy conservation mode" when it was clear I was in an organizational situation which intended to suck me dry rather than to support me. In order to survive I learned how to become withdrawn. I also learned how to simply work to targets and nothing else. Interestingly, I had been warned that this may be the case by a diversity practitioner in the City of London.

According to her account, she too had started off enthusiastically, full of ideas, and yet found that most of her energy had been usurped. She had advised me not to be so "ambitious." At first I was saddened by her advice. Over time I realized it was the only way to survive in a hierarchical system that was purely compliance-driven and which was not versed in moral and ethical responsibility to stakeholders. Sad to say, I learned to be an under-achiever, according to my own personal and professional standards, even though on paper I had reached and at times exceeded my organizational targets. The end result is organizations breeding mediocrity, not encouraging excellence.

Sitting in isolation

I had no team of which I was a part. The organizational chart had me reporting to the vice principal of quality but I was not part of the quality team which held weekly meetings. It took some time to realize this and, when I did, I had to ask to be included in quality meetings at the start of 2009/2010. It was agreed I would be, although this never transpired.

There was no feasible way for me to achieve improvements in the diversity management and social justice performance as one manager, sitting alone within a large and very complex organization. I had no budget; I had no staff to manage. In short, I had no infrastructure to enable anything significant to happen. I knew then I had to find creative ways to find human resource support as well as finances to achieve my vision. It was time to use my business skills in order to keep the ship afloat.

I realized I needed a team, so in 2009/2010 the working groups were formally started. I was, at this time, granted an administrative assistant who would help me with organizing groups and activities of groups. I appreciated this resource very much, as it provided me with a better infrastructure for action. Together, she and I organized the collective action that was to take place in 2009/2010 through the working groups and committee.

Does anyone understand what I'm doing?

I was doing what I felt needed to be done, based upon information and feedback, but I had yet to find a way of communicating this in a simplistic way to others. I was more than happy with the complex system in place, allowing for co-creating, self-organization etc., but others were not entirely clear about what was taking place. The best way to clarify, I felt, was to create a visual diagram, using corporate language to which people were accustomed.

As I was under the quality umbrella, I thought it was best to work with the director of quality in order to come up with a model consistent with his model of quality. He helped me put the theoretical foundations of my work into diagram form; together we designed the Diversity Quality Cycle, which represents the governance structure I had devised with my co-researchers in 2008/2009. So, by December 2009, I had codified the complex governance cycle that was already up and running and in full operation. This was well received by internal and external stakeholders and partners.

Board Members need to be a part of the Diversity Quality Cycle

Initially in the Diversity Quality Cycle, there was a complete gap in communication between Board members and working groups. I considered this gap may be responsible for misunderstandings, and also continued isolation of governors understanding daily business operations of the college.

While it was stated governors should not "interfere" with the running of day-to-day business, this did not mean they should be divorced from it altogether. It was clear that Board members had very little knowledge of equality, diversity, and inclusion, which made it nearly impossible for them, as a governing body, to lead according to key principles. In order to bridge this gap I invited governors to be part of working groups of their choice. They were invited to attend meetings as observers and/or contributors. Only one governor showed an interest in doing so; she was female and the only governor with a minority ethnic background. She could also be categorized as disabled.

Industrial military complex

I found the wider governance of the corporation to still be reflective of this old-school military industrial complex. There were high levels of aggression and pressure to deliver. While I am not averse to either of these, it was my profound experience that more emphasis was put upon results than upon processes by which results are achieved.

Conflict existed between achieving greater social justice, protecting the reputation and keeping to the rank and file of the college. There were times in which the importance of acting upon my conscience was far greater than protecting the reputation of the corporation. Outspoken in this way, I experienced being "disciplined" for behaving in accordance with my principles, principles that were central to my role as equality and diversity manager.

As my first line manager would say, I was accustomed to acting as a consultant. I had to stop now I was "employed" and had to act according to rank and file. This somehow suggested a form of separation of management from non-management, something that I felt created difficulties in the first instance. Eventually, I "did what I was told" or asked to do.

If people required a report or a presentation they received it from me. I removed my passion and eventually my will to transfer knowledge to my "superiors." I removed my personal opinion. I simply just "did my job" and nothing more. I felt in order to survive I had to become "mediocre" according to my own standards.

I continued to try to achieve ambitious tasks, with high-profile people and events. But I also knew the college was not ready and, even at times, undeserving of such affiliation. It was indeed provincial, though it tried to give the impression of being international in its outlook and culture. This could not have been further from the truth.

I was able to establish a fair amount of support and engagement from stakeholders. There were people who were very eager to participate. There were people whose values were reflected in the words I created for the corporate website, words which were consistent with my own personal values. There was a high level of enthusiasm, particularly by the end of my first year in post. We rode this momentum and were able to create an incredibly impactful public community event in January 2010. While very tangible, it was not possible to sustain this momentum.

Can't get a word in edgeways

With the non-transparent departure of my direct line manager, who no longer chaired the senior leadership team, my senior leadership support waned. The group chair was taken over by the vice principal of corporate resources, a "hierarchist" who deemed it inappropriate for the staff development manager and me, the equality and diversity manager, to be on senior leadership group alongside directors and senior executives. This change I found offensive and demoralizing. I began to feel exploited and not appreciated for my talents. Thus, my personal employment experience was already running counter to the values of equality, diversity, and inclusion. I knew I was in the wrong place.

Shortly after this change in group structure, the staff development manager resigned. I did not. I decided at this point to give the senior leadership group and members of the Board only what they asked of me, nothing more and nothing less. I was "invited" to group leadership team meetings once a month. The first two I attended, I was given the time and space to present mere snapshots without any true knowledge exchange. The result of this was that I simply stopped talking. In order to be more politically effective, I learned to speak when I was spoken to. My job had become tediously boring; my spirit and voice had become squelched.

Stop going to management meetings

My direct line manager left the organization in March 2010. He had chaired a quality curriculum management group as well. I had supported him weekly in these meetings, but after I had been ejected from the senior leadership group, taking into consideration the finite amount of time and energy I had, I decided that attending these meetings would be counter-productive for my own agenda. I would dedicate myself to work within the community with my colleagues, students, and community partners.

Executive and senior leaders met every Wednesday morning on the organization's largest site. This left no management or leadership presence on any of the other sites across the county. I decided I would be more useful staying on my main campus during management meeting times in order to support my colleagues there and on other campuses in responding to any day-to-day equality, diversity, and inclusion issues that arose. My absence from such meetings was never addressed, nor was I ever disciplined or reprimanded for not attending management meetings; this reinforced my management redundancy within the context of the corporation. I was happy no longer playing the game, as I found I was more effective as a practitioner without the burden of those management meetings.

Such meetings were generally viewed by managers themselves to be too long, too dull, too mechanistic, and too fruitless. There was no point my sitting there for hours, only to be given the floor for no more than 5 minutes within the course of a 2-hour meeting. This was highly ineffective for others and me.

I decided to devote myself to the working groups, which were designed to support a key director in their main area of business responsibility, taking a very strong bottom-up approach to the change process at this point. I was no longer going to be the "trophy" equality and diversity mouthpiece of the organization. Directors could and should by now be able to be conversant about equality, diversity, and inclusion within the context of their business areas, and able to table and pass whatever motions were necessary in order for progress to be made.

Making governance fun

The quality of exchange and engagement taking place within working groups, which could be defined as: informal, yet professional; creative; highly energetic; and enjoyable, was not translating to the quality of exchange and engagement in the Diversity and Inclusivity Committee meetings when chaired by the chief executive. I found it fascinating that most members of the committee had direct experience of the positive dynamics of working groups, yet they fell into this corporate mold of rank and file and what could be defined as sterile governance of a highly dynamic and volatile subject area. I found attending committee meetings excruciating at times and really did not enjoy my own involvement in the committee.

When the principal asked me to take over as chair, I decided I had a commitment to myself, and all of my other co-researchers, to ensure the spirit of working group meetings found its way into the spirit of committee meetings. I was constantly fighting what seemed like inevitable losing battles.

End of story

By the end of the research, I found I was carrying all sorts of corporate titles and labels. They included equality and diversity management, corporate responsibility and business development manager, chair of the Diversity and Inclusivity Committee and chair of the Sustainability Committee. Yet, none of these titles carried any real responsibility or clout. I had possessed no real influential powers on the core organizational culture and its overriding ethos (low diversity and ethical climate).

I had no budgets from which to work in order to make it possible to achieve goals set out in the vision and medium-term plan. Functioning as a figurehead was very unattractive and completely hypocritical in my estimation, once again making it difficult for me to achieve the vision around achievable and sustainable improvements in social justice. Actually, I learned, more than anything, that I do not wish to be a diversity practitioner in an organization that is not driven by a social justice agenda, and that does not have a strong ethical climate.

Summary and conclusions

There are five conclusions at which I arrived by the end of the action research case study. I learned:

1   To remove myself from leadership and management conversations as my voice had been primarily muted.
2   I personally cannot function best within a hierarchical system that is driven purely by compliance.
3   Education as I knew it was nowhere to be found within the organization, and that the organization had much more potential to do harm than good than I had understood at the beginning.
4   As a social entrepreneur, it is essential to work within organizations upholding the values I have as an individual; lip service is very damaging, demoralizing, and stripping.
5   It was time to go back to running my own company.

Many things changed throughout my time initially as equality and diversity manager. We certainly improved systems, particularly around the collection of demographic data. We built stronger partnerships with the local authority and with the police and community groups. We threw a few good parties, which helped to develop a sense of community spirit. We made a bit of money through the sale of educational qualifications.

From an equalities point of view, many things did not change. There was no increase in the number of staff members who define themselves as Black and minority ethnic; there certainly was a decrease in management over time, as the director of finance and I both left and were the only two minority ethnic managers. There was no increase in the number of staff members who considered themselves disabled. The college did not come to grips with the notion of sexual orientation or religion. There were still strong gender divides within faculties and curriculum areas. Flexible working within further education and family-friendly policies seemed to be a complete impossibility. Long-work hours culture seemed to be prevalent; overworking was the default mode. In addition, with much less financial remuneration for one's time and with the increase of redundancies and workloads, the level of demoralization peaked.

As I reflect upon all of these changes and stagnations, I am reminded of systemic barriers to social change and social justice. I am reminded that nothing can take place within isolation, and that organizations that host diversity management strategies have got to be more values-driven, not just financially and legally-driven. This is most certainly the case when organizations are organized according to rigid, controlling hierarchies and, second, are reactionary in addressing and attempting to solve problems. It felt as though I was in a place that was sprinting at top speed to stay in last place, while spinning the rhetoric of excellence. Where did this leave me?

I did not wish to reinforce the status quo and to continue to be a part of my own subjugation. I certainly did not wish to be seen by others as part of the status quo, whether they were the managers or the managed within the organization. So, it left me faced with the challenge of creating an ideal organizational leadership culture through my own company. It is here where I have the power and the agency to model the attitudes and behaviors that I saw were so profoundly lacking in the leadership and management of the case study organization.

It left me more firmly committed to facilitating and being part of long-term changes in social justice. It left me not wishing to be stuck within mediocrity. It reinforced the risk-taker in me, and my commitment to working with organizations that have a leadership willing to challenge and change the status quo.

How to be a better diversity and inclusion practitioner, for me, personally, is very much dependent upon the environment within which one is given to either succeed, or in some instances to fail. How do I improve my practice? I do this by making sure I work within an organization balanced in its approach to social justice, respecting all three diversity management frameworks (equality, diversity, and inclusion). It is important to choose organizations which respect the Rule of Law, and which are primarily driven not by profit, but by a mature sense of the moral responsibility organizations have to society. Where and with whom one chooses to work is essential if those feelings of "energy conservation" and exploitation are to be avoided, if we are to ensure our spirits are not robbed from us in order to serve the status quo. It is a form of enslavement that I found I was not prepared to endure.

I remember that, at the initial job interview in July 2008, I was asked what I would do if people did not support the diversity management agenda. I said then that if values have been expressed as something important to organization, I would hold myself and others to account. I said it then, and meant it. I did it, and found I was not so popular. I was not concerned about my unpopularity at all, and found I was not willing to be co-opted and held to ransom for my monthly pay check. I said it then, and I would say it again. As with many jobs and roles, people wanted me to do what they wanted me to do, not what I could do, or what needed to be done.

All diversity management practice is housed within a wider host organization. It has been part of my experience, and the experience of others, that many organizations within which we work actually reject the idea of diversity management in full practice, and are not "walking the talk." This may be one of the main reasons for the categorical failure of diversity management strategies and initiatives to achieve long-term and sustainable change.

As in biology, we find ourselves as diversity practitioners in a situation in which our host rejects us, similar to a host rejecting an organ transplant. While good things are achieved within stakeholder communities on a local level, macro governance of the diversity management agenda has remained weak. Too many senior executives and leaders remained detached, separated, and disengaged from the critical mass of employees. This is potentially a vital factor in the overall ineffectiveness of the diversity management.

Having had my own personal action experience of being an in-house diversity and inclusion professional, I conducted a small questionnaire study of other diversity and inclusion professionals so that I could compare and contrast my experiences with theirs. The data collected from this study is presented in chapter 11.

10 The dynamics of the Diversity Quality Cycle

> Quality is never an accident; it is always the result of high intention, sincere effort, intelligent direction and skillful execution; it represents the wise choice of many alternatives.
>
> —William A. Foster

The action research case study in the previous chapter examined the utility of the Diversity Quality Cycle, which can be instrumental in facilitating a process of substantial shifts in the social justice outcomes within organizations. In addition, the Diversity Quality Cycle provides a diversity management framework through which improvements in ethical decision-making can be achieved. It provides a mechanism for capturing and for acting upon the views and opinions of a diverse and representative body of stakeholders in order to create improved diversity management outcomes.

The Diversity Quality Cycle is a tool that may be used beyond the purposes of traditional diversity management. While my main focus has been upon diversity management practices, the Diversity Quality Cycle, as a system of innovative and egalitarian governance, can and should be used as a framework for cultural transformations of any type, regardless of the subject matter. For instance, it could be used for change management around health and safety, customer support, or even the introduction and integration of new technologies within a business.

The Diversity Quality Cycle provides a framework designed to capture a diversity of stakeholder opinions and perspectives, and to integrate this information into decision-making processes of a given organization. Thus, it is envisaged, by applying the Diversity Quality Cycle, ethical and egalitarian decision-making can be significantly improved and as a result so too can social justice performance.

Applying the Diversity Quality Cycle within organizational settings

Diversity management literature highlighted that diversity management practice, in particular diversity training, has been only somewhat effective, and is often ineffective. This literature presents a picture of the inadequacy of diversity management practices and explains why diversity management practices may be only marginally successful. The results of the action research study presented in the previous chapters support this. The results suggest there is need for the Diversity Quality Cycle as a framework of ethical governance and positive change within organizations. However, the results also show how difficult it is to introduce and sustain this level of complex governance.

The study highlights several impediments that must be addressed and rectified if diversity management performance is to improve. The data show organizational diversity management strategies may be less effective when diversity management is driven primarily by compliance; exists within purely hierarchical cultures; is seen primarily as a necessary requirement; focuses upon strands of equality only, with no or low focus on inclusion; and lacks an engaged and exemplary senior leadership.

The Diversity Quality Cycle functions in a way that enables all of the above barriers to be overcome, in order to support a more effective change management process. It offers a framework of democratic stakeholder engagement, in which senior leaders are included within the category of employee stakeholders, thus attempting to avoid negative impacts of top-down leadership. While acknowledging the importance and the need for hierarchy, the Diversity Quality Cycle advocates democratic engagement and dialog. It, therefore, does not attempt to create a "flat" system of organizational governance in which everyone is considered to be "equal." It purports the concept of polyarchy ("many rule"). This polyarchical system enables a greater distribution of influence and power among stakeholders while still maintaining hierarchy where and when appropriate.

The Diversity Quality Cycle is designed to operate according to what are believed to be optimal internal organizational conditions, within which effective diversity management can take place. It is understood there is always a place for hierarchy, legal compliance, and addressing the concerns of all equality strands. On the strength of this idea, I advocate a pluralistic approach to diversity management and governance. Corporate motivation should be moral, legal, and financial, as there is corporate responsibility on all levels. Organizational culture should be hierarchical, flexible, and entrepreneurial. I would hold that leadership, as stakeholders, should always be engaged. I would also hold that diversity management needs to be seen both as a "necessary license to operate" and as an "asset which adds value," and no matter what, should be driven by inclusive, engaged leaders with a commitment to social justice and a seasoned moral imperative.

If the pre-conditions do not exist, then an organization may wish to commit first to redressing any structural organizational inadequacies and institutional barriers which may obstruct the effective execution of a diversity management strategy. If an organization cannot commit to this, then it may be facing further wastage of resources through an exercise that may be perceived as paying "lip service" to the values of equality, diversity, and inclusion. In addition, application of the Diversity Quality Cycle may not yield the "desired" results of improvements of social justice within an organization.

The Diversity Quality Cycle alone cannot succeed in bringing about long-term sustainable change within organizations; there are very strong internal and external factors that contribute to the determination of success. If an organization does not reflect principles and values of the Diversity Quality Cycle internally, then sustainable change may be more difficult to achieve. It has to be a living model in which there are high levels of collective stakeholder engagement and dialog; these are key ingredients to ensuring the Diversity Quality Cycle is effective as a model.

The case study demonstrated this in particular. It also showed how difficult it was to deconstruct the operational hierarchy within the context of a public sector United Kingdom organization, in order to enable stakeholders to make a fairer and more balanced contribution to the success of the organization. The results of the In-House

Diversity Practitioner survey, that appears in the next chapter, support this by showing that the public sector operates much less effectively than the private sector which tends to have more competitive and collaborate cultures.

It is argued here that internal integrity (ethic climate) of the wider organizational culture must be intact in order for the Diversity Quality Cycle to work effectively, or an organization must be committed to improving its inadequacies as part of the Diversity Quality Cycle execution. If it is, then an organization is more likely to make fair and ethical decisions in light of, and sometimes despite, external pressures and changes.

Despite surrounding circumstances, the intervention which was put in place (the application of the Diversity Quality Cycle) did yield demonstrably positive results, for individuals who were directly involved in the action research project, and for the organization itself, however, was it possible to achieve sustainable outcomes. Despite this result, it is still believed that the Diversity Quality Cycle has the ability to provide the foundation and framework for social change and improvements in social justice outcomes. Future research can be focused upon how best to apply and utilize the Diversity Quality Cycle in order to achieve greater sustainability of social change and social justice within organizations.

The close collaboration between practitioners and researchers continues to be vital, and should be a part of on-going work in this field. What must be borne in mind, particularly within the public sector during this time of economic austerity, is the rapid disappearance of competent equality and diversity practitioners. Thus, if work begun in many places is to continue, it is essential researchers work directly with key business professionals who remain.

While I believe the Diversity Quality Cycle has the ability to enable diversity practitioners, and the organizations, to improve upon performance, it is also clear it is necessary to have collective buy-in from all of those who participate in the cycle. Applying the Diversity Quality Cycle in the absence of clear, shared collective objectives, in the absence of knowledge and skills among senior leaders, and in isolation from core governance structures may continue to prove ineffective.

Further research is needed to explore the extent to which the Diversity Quality Cycle has the ability to help transform organizational cultures. More longitudinal studies are required in order to establish if, by approaching equality and diversity with this innovative governance strategy, social justice outcomes can be improved within organizations.

I believe it is a viable mechanism of transformation, which, if developed further, has far-reaching capabilities within the global marketplace. Future research should continue to explore how to embed equality, diversity, and inclusion into organizational structure and leadership culture. In addition, as sustainability is a key concern going forward, future research must continue to be longitudinal in nature.

There is wide scope for exploring diversity management and change management practices within businesses further. However, as businesses operate within, and are microcosms of, our larger civic society, there is also a need for researchers and practitioners to turn their attention to wider civic society. We must, as responsible professionals, address some fundamental challenges within the civic arena that impact upon business behavior.

Applying the Diversity Quality Cycle within civic society

As volatility within the global marketplace continues, and sustainability and economic survivability becomes increasingly important to social capital, future research must help to find ways of preserving the value of social capital that is currently under serious threat.

Diversity management practices of today were born out of popular civil rights uprisings of the 1960s and 1970s. The main focus upon this civil unrest was the institutional oppression of women and minority ethnic communities in particular. It highlighted historic and deep-seated inequalities that subjugated certain members of society, members who were also denied rights associated to full citizenship. Over the years, this struggle has come to envelope causes of groups such as disabled, gay, lesbian and bisexual, religious, transgendered, and economically disadvantaged individuals, all of whom have valid concerns about their continued societal marginalization.

The anti-discrimination legislation has become more complex as it continues to include additional social categories within its list of protected characteristics. Despite the raft of legislation to guide human behavior inside and outside of corporate settings, we have seen some social justice improvements for certain minority groups. We have not, however, witnessed real fundamental changes in the way in which organizations, corporations, or governments govern themselves and their citizens and stakeholders. The ultimate corporate power structure (i.e. managerialist capitalism) has remained in operation.

This research has been conducted in a time of great economic, political, and social turbulence; much of this turbulence is still present. In some cases it is intensifying, as further economic cuts are sought and further re-structuring and redundancies are to come. Some argue Western democracy and the economic system upon which it relies (predatory capitalism) are arguably defunct.

Academic action researchers, in particular, can play a much needed and valuable hand in helping society make the transition from old to new. It is argued here, due to the severity of the current socio-economic crisis, we researchers should turn our attention first and foremost to concerns of wider civic society. If we are to be socially responsible in our practice—and ethics dictate we must be—then we must work together with our local and global partners to help facilitate and guide a global change process. We can begin by exploring further application and utility of the Diversity Quality Cycle within civic society. The idea of "collaborative capitalism" is a very attractive one. The question arises: "How do we get those in a position of power to collaborate?"

We are confronted with very large challenges, for which there appear to be neither viable solutions, nor textbook answers. What is required is creativity and imagination of people who are dedicated to working together. Traditional demarcations of race, gender, disability, sexual orientation, academic, practitioner, corporate executive, civil servant, etc., are now secondary to the need of working collectively to redress institutional socio-economic inequality. The Diversity Quality Cycle provides a framework for improving democratic dialog and ethical decision-making, and can be used by researchers, practitioners, business professionals, and politicians as they work toward improving social justice outcomes for all stakeholders within society.

Applying the Diversity Quality Cycle cross-culturally

The Anglo-American model of diversity management has been exported and been imposed upon a variety of cultures which do not possess the same legal, cultural, or moral context as the Anglo-American model. In the absence of a high level of cross-cultural competence, indiscriminately applying an Anglo-American diversity management framework has rendered many a global diversity and inclusion strategy illegitimate, inadequate, and ineffective. More research in this area needs to be conducted outside Anglo–American and Continental European governance structures and value systems. This is of particular importance as these Western economies have lost their global economic strongholds.

There is sparse research of this nature emanating from regions such as Brazil, Russia, India, China, and South Africa (BRICSA). Now is an opportune time to see greater collaboration between researchers across regions, in order to generate a more global picture and a greater comprehension of global dynamics at play. There is scope for considering dimensions of national culture, highlighted in the work of Geert Hofstede.[1]

His work pays particular attention to power distance (an acceptance of hierarchical order in which everybody has a place and which needs no further justification versus a desire to equalize the distribution of power and demand justification for inequalities of power); individualism versus collectivism (individuals are expected to take care of only themselves and their immediate families—its opposite, collectivism, represents a preference for a tightly-knit framework in society in which individuals can expect their relatives or members of a particular in–group to look after them in exchange for unquestioning loyalty); masculinity versus femininity ("tough versus tender" cultures); uncertainty avoidance (how a society deals with the fact that the future can never be known); long–term orientation (maintaining time-honored traditions or encouraging modern education as a way to prepare for the future); and indulgence versus constraint (allowing for free gratification or suppressing gratification).

Given the extent to which there is huge volatility, ambiguity, and uncertainty within the current global marketplace, it may be that certain cultures and their economies show a greater capacity to maintain higher power distances between people, to act collectively, and to engage in long–term planning, and are therefore more likely to survive in such circumstances. Those who have less flexibility and long–term planning may show signs of struggling to compete and to survive. The BRICSA nations may reflect the former, while Anglo–American and Continental European countries may reflect the latter according to Hofstede's framework.

Future research into diversity management should, therefore, explore different approaches to equality, diversity, and inclusion, as they exist within and between Anglo–American, Western European, and BRICSA cultural contexts. Attention should also be paid to ways in which issues of equality, diversity, and inclusion evolve within the Next Eleven—N-11 (Bangladesh, Egypt, Indonesia, Iran, Mexico, Nigeria, Pakistan, Philippines, South Korea, Turkey, and Vietnam).

Hofstede's work can provide a meaningful foundation for exploring the relationship between dominant leadership styles as dictated by wider cultural contexts, and the extent to which these styles either help to facilitate or hinder equality of opportunity and valuing of diversity within the contexts of organizational and business development.

The purpose of this book is to explore various variables contributing to the ineffectiveness of diversity management, and options to improve the effectiveness of diversity management strategies and their outcomes. As companies expand globally, it is important to generate knowledge that sheds light on this deficiency and provides practitioners and researchers with the knowledge and tools to improve upon corporate performance. If this is not done, then diversity management practice will continue to be the waste of time, energy, money, and commitment it has proven to be thus far as a management control tool.

It is important to address the inadequacies of diversity management within Anglo-American cultural contexts. There is much that can be learned and improved by learning from other cultures. The Justice Index and the Rule of Law Index both highlighted cross-cultural differences, and the challenges these differences present in managing diversity within certain cultural contexts. It is my hope that the future holds in store an intensification of global efforts between diversity management researchers and practitioners. We have a very real and immediate challenge, as researchers and practitioners, to ensure the importance of this agenda does not slip away in light of global economic pressures, and that we develop greater global collaborations that will enable us to make better sense of this very complex global picture of equality, diversity, and inclusion.

If global diversity is to be managed better, it is essential to understand and find solutions to challenges within Western cultures, and not to continue to impose diversity frameworks and models, that do not even work in the West, into non-Western societies which operate within different cultural frameworks. If we fail to arrive at this understanding and to make the appropriate cultural adjustments, diversity management practices run the risk of perpetuating social injustice rather than improving it.

Diversity management success requires engaged leadership

The Diversity Quality Cycle, an participative governance model, is based upon the principles of the Rule of Law, that upholds the value of social justice, equality, and inclusion. It is a significant contribution to knowledge in the field of diversity management. As the architect of this model, I drew from literature highlighting the positive impact of stakeholder engagement theory in improving business performance and from complexity theory. I applied the tenets of both to diversity management practice, and have attempted to demonstrate ways in which diversity management performance can be improved through the application of the Diversity Quality Cycle. While the results of the study yielded some very positive outcomes, none of the outcomes were sustainable. I explored factors such as corporate motivation, perceptions of diversity, corporate culture, and senior executive engagement as possible barriers to successful diversity management.

This will enable practitioners to avoid the application of deficient, ineffective models in cultures, particularly cultures with emerging markets. The way in which organizations are governed plays a huge role in the effectiveness of diversity management strategies. This book has argued in favor of governance structures which are ethical, participative, and egalitarian in nature, and in line with the value of equality, diversity and inclusion.

Participative governance is essential if organizations wish to run responsibly and ethically, not just consulting with stakeholders, but working together with stakeholders in building corporate cultures that support corporate values. I attach a very serious health warning about organizations merely engaging in diversity management in order to comply with legislation or to maximize profit. Diversity management cannot be a success in morally bankrupt leadership and organizations.

Ethical, engaged, and enlightened leadership is paramount. We need leaders who are driven by their company's values and who lead by example in the business areas. Senior executives need to take the time to understand and engage with others. If they are not prepared to do this, then they are not prepared to enable their organizations to transform and to develop; they are certainly not prepared to liberate people and improve the quality of the lives of employees.

From the past, there is also a lingering belief among many that cultural transformation in the direction of greater equality and social justice is a slow process. Those of us who are older can "remember when" things were nowhere as advanced as they are today. We are aware, and have lived first-hand, the length of time it has taken to get as far as we have gotten. But there are many of us, particularly younger people, who do not accept the argument that change has to be a long, drawn-out process.

Looking critically at the past, it did take many years to change legislation, to give people the right to vote and to be active members of liberal democracies, and to create access to higher education for aspiring communities. We have created the building blocks of social justice that enable people to have greater access to inalienable rights. But, we have to ask ourselves, once we have laid such solid foundations, why are significant improvements in social justice outcomes taking so long?

This may be because the "Rule by Law" has been an overwhelming popular approach to diversity management, reflected in the primarily top-down managerialism. It may also be because, in the absence of fundamental and equity at the core of this management approach, substantial and sustainable improvements in social justice outcomes are unachievable. It is argued here that if businesses adopt participative governance systems that are based on organizational equity and engaged leadership then organizational cultures can transform into those governed by the "Rule of Law" if we are to change the landscape of social justice outcomes.

With over 40 years of investing in and creating a plethora of capable and highly qualified (and often overqualified) people from historical minority groups (i.e. women, disabled people, and minority ethnic people), why are there still so few in these positions of power, compared to their historically privileged counterparts?

Meanwhile, there are others, those who may have had certain privileges afforded to them in the past, and who may feel as though the ground is slipping away from under their feet, who feel that equal opportunities are working against them and stripping them of their positions and future opportunities, comparative to their "minority counterparts." It is further unhelpful when this population of workers feels aggrieved at being labeled "racists," "sexists," "homophobes," and other such likes. A diversity management impasse has been created and needs to be handled wisely and skillfully.

Why are we still looking around innumerable organizations and continuing to see a dearth of women and minority ethnic senior leaders? It is not as though capable and competent individuals from diverse backgrounds do not exist in the lower echelons of the very same organizations. It not as though we have not created a critical mass of educated people from diverse backgrounds who are skilled at leading. The talent is there. So why then is it taking so long for this talent to rise up the ranks?

Current diversity management models and practices are dominated by legal and economic discourses. Their existence appears to many to be symbolic. As they skirt around key institutional power relations and barriers that create them, their ability to reconfigure this world is rendered impotent. It is time to dismantle this form of diversity management. This does not mean "throwing the baby away with the bath water," so to speak. There are many things that are useful about our current theories and practices. It is just that the roots are not strong or healthy enough to sustain us currently or in the future. What is missing is the ethical, moral dimension that needs to be at the core of any activity around social justice.

In the next chapter, I explore, through a questionnaire study, the experiences of diversity and inclusion practitioners who are working, or who have worked, as full-time employees within an organizational sector. Having had a lived experience as such a practitioner within the action research study presented earlier, it was important to capture my peers' perceptions of how effective they felt they were being as diversity and inclusion professionals, and how effective they felt their overall diversity management initiatives were. I wanted to begin to tease out some of the key barriers to progress that I believe were revealed and highlighted in the action research study. Though the questionnaire sample size is small, what emerges from the next study is a much clearer picture of the types of enabling and disabling conditions that contribute to the effectiveness of diversity management strategies and initiatives.

Note

1 Retrieved June 17, 2015 from http://citeseerx.ist.psu.edu/viewdoc/download?doi=10.1.1.446. 3598&rep=rep1&type=pdf.

11 A world according to some diversity and inclusion professionals

Co-opted convictions will always betray you.

—Charles M. Blow

With the Diversity Quality Cycle in mind, I wanted to get a view of how diversity and inclusion professionals assessed their corporate cultures and their roles within those cultures. I conducted a questionnaire study to test the waters. This chapter reviews the results of this questionnaire study. It gives us a snapshot of how some diversity and inclusion professionals view their organizations, their effectiveness within their organizations, and their satisfaction with their roles. While the sample size is small, nonetheless, it provides a sketch of the field from upon which we can elaborate in the future.

A survey of in-house diversity practitioners within the United Kingdom and Europe was conducted in order to ascertain what key variables, if any, might be limiting the effectiveness of diversity management. The questionnaire explored the extent to which diversity management strategies have been successful (the dependent variable), and if there was any correlation between it, and several independent variables, which were as follows: business sector; corporate motivation; corporate culture; senior leadership engagement; organizational equity; and perceptions of organizational diversity.

The results of the survey are presented, analyzed, interpreted, and discussed. The limitations of the research are explored and further research directions are suggested.

Methodology

An online questionnaire was designed for completion by in-house diversity practitioners. Personal networks and social networking media sources were used to advertise the questionnaire and to invite people to complete it.

Sampling

There were 34 respondents who started the survey, and 31 respondents who completed 100 percent of the survey. Of those 31 respondents, 85 percent were diversity practitioners, 15 percent had been practitioners in the past, 65 percent of respondents represented the private sector, 24 percent represented the public sector, 3 percent represented the third sector, and 8 percent represented other sectors that included representative bodies and housing.

All respondents were based within the United Kingdom and Europe; a majority was based in the United Kingdom, with one respondent from Spain and another from Germany. Respondents were asked to identify if they were from the private, public, or third sector, and also given the choice to choose "other." The majority of respondents (20), were from private sector organizations. Eight respondents were from the public sector; one was from the third sector; three said other. As representation from the third sector and other sectors is significantly low, the main analysis of this data is focused upon private and public sector organizations.

Ninety-one percent of respondents worked in an organization that had a formal diversity policy in place. Ninety-seven percent carried out specific diversity initiatives to support their organization's diversity policy, 88 percent of respondents worked in an organization with 500 or more employees, 9 percent work within small to medium enterprises (SMEs), 3 percent identified being part of business networks.

Data collection

Respondents were asked to complete an online questionnaire consisting of multiple choice and open-ended qualitative questions.

Measures

The dependent variable was diversity practitioners' perception of their organization's diversity management strategy effectiveness.

Six independent variables were measured: business sector; corporate motivation; corporate culture; level of senior leadership engagement; level of organizational equity; and organizational perception of diversity.

Results

Benchmark for effectiveness of diversity management

Respondents were asked to rate the overall effectiveness of their organization's diversity management strategy. They were asked to rate performance based on a 7-point scale of: "very effective" (1), "effective" (2), "somewhat effective" (3), neither effective nor ineffective" (4), "somewhat ineffective" (5), "ineffective" (6), and very ineffective" (7).

Three percent of respondents said "very effective," 32 percent said "effective," 48 percent said "somewhat effective," 10 percent said "neither effective nor ineffective," 3 percent said "somewhat ineffective," 3 percent said "very ineffective." Overall, the effectiveness of diversity management strategies was 2.90. On a 7-point scale this puts the score at "somewhat effective" bordering on "effective," showing only average, to slightly above average results.

The baseline data on overall perceptions of the diversity management strategy were explored in relation, and disaggregated according to the independent variables: business sector; corporate motivation; corporate culture; level of senior leadership engagement; level of organizational equity; and organizational perception of diversity.

Business sector

Hypothesis 1—Diversity management strategies are more effective within private sector organizations.

The hypothesis here was that private sector organizations would outperform public sector organizations, on the basis that private sectors organizations were more motivated by a business case for diversity, rather by legal compliance.

There were 20 respondents from the private sector and eight from the public sector. In addition, three respondents represented "third sector" and "other sector." The data here show the difference in performance between private and public sector organizations, showing private sector organizations outperforming public sector organizations.

Based on a 7-point scale (1 = very effective to 7 = very ineffective), within private sector organizations: 5 percent said their strategy was "very effective," 40 percent said "effective," 35 percent said "somewhat effective," 15 percent said "neither effective nor ineffective," 5 percent said "somewhat ineffective." The mean was 2.75 and standard deviation is 0.97.

Within public sector organizations: 0 percent said "very effective," 25 percent said "effective," 63 percent said "somewhat effective," 0 percent said "neither ineffective nor effective," 0 percent said "somewhat ineffective," 0 percent said "ineffective," and 12 percent said "very ineffective." The mean is 3.25 with a standard deviation of 1.58.

While there is not a vastly marked difference between private and public sectors, the data nonetheless shows weaker performance within the public sector. Remaining data explore potential differences between private and public sector organizations that may contribute to variations in diversity management performance.

Corporate motivation

Hypothesis 2—Diversity management strategies are more effective in organizations motivated by a moral imperative.

The diversity literature addresses three cases that argue in favor of diversity. They are the legal case, the business case, and the moral case. According to this framework, respondents were asked to identify the primary motivation for their organization's diversity management strategy. The choices were legal compliance, profit maximization and moral responsibility. "Other" was offered as an additional category in order to capture motivations not yet identified formally in the literature.

Thirty-six percent of companies were motivated by legal compliance, 31 percent were motivated by profit optimization, 6 percent were motivated by moral responsibility, 27 percent were motivated by something "other" which included staff engagement, reputation management, service delivery, senior leadership support, creativity and compliance, talent shortages, research, and developing tools to help other companies.

The data was disaggregated by sector motivation. Within the private sector, 23 percent were motivated by legal compliance, 50 percent by profit maximization, 9 percent by moral responsibility and 18 percent other (identified as staff engagement, leadership support, profit and compliance and talent shortages). There appear to be a significant number of "other" choices, as more people choose this category than the "moral responsibility" category.

Within the public sector, 88 percent of public sector organizations were motivated by legal compliance, 0 percent by profit maximization, 0 percent by moral responsibility and 12 percent by something other (identified as a driver for creativity and compliance).

When corporate motivation was cross-tabulated with overall effectiveness of diversity management strategy the results were that two respondents who reported the corporate motivation being moral responsibility said their strategies were "very effective" and "effective." Those primarily motivated by profit maximization reported their diversity management strategies were "effective." While those primarily motivated by legal compliance reported a majority of diversity management strategies are "somewhat effective."

"Other" motivations (which included membership expectation, staff engagement, external profile, improving service performance, customer satisfaction, combination of legal and profit, combination of creativity and compliance, and the development of research tools to provide support to companies) were all reported as being "somewhat effective."

Moral responsibility results were favorable, however, since the number of respondents in this category was so significantly low, the data could not support the hypothesis that organizations motivated primarily by moral responsibility will have more effective diversity management strategies. What was disappointing was that so few diversity and inclusion professionals report working for companies that had a strong moral motivation. This did not bode well for them working within organizations that had strong ethical climates. The statistical significance was seen with organizations that were motivated primarily by "legal compliance" and "profit maximization."

Dominant corporate culture

> Hypothesis 3—Diversity management strategies are more effective in flexible and collaborative organizational cultures.

The questionnaire explored the quality of the corporate culture within which diversity management initiatives are taking place. Respondents were given the choice between controlling/hierarchical; competitive/market-driven; collaborative/flexible; creative/entrepreneurial; and other. The results were that 41 percent said their organizations were "controlling/hierarchical," 26 percent said "market-driven," 24 percent said "collaborative/flexible," 6 percent said "creative/entrepreneurial," 3 percent said "other," which was defined as "flexible" depending on with whom you work, but that "the overall hierarchy had a different set of rules for senior people who operate outside company policy, openly and unapologetically."

The dominant corporate culture was then compared to overall diversity management effectiveness. Results below suggest that when an organization was more flexible/collaborative, diversity management strategies were more effective.

Diversity management strategies seem to be most effective when the organizational culture was "flexible/collaborative" (mean = 2.43). Followed by organizational cultures that were "competitive/market-driven" (mean = 2.75). In both cases, diversity management is still considered to be "effective." When organizational cultures were controlling/hierarchical (mean = 3.23), the diversity management strategy was seen to be "somewhat effective." While a majority of organizations had controlling/hierarchical cultures, data supports the hypothesis that collaborative/flexible organizational cultures had more effective diversity management strategies.

This data was disaggregated and analyzed according to private and public sector performance. Because of the low response rate of the third sector and other sectors, they were not included within the analysis.

Within the private sector, 36 percent were "controlling/hierarchical," 36 percent were "competitive/market-driven," 23 percent were "collaborative/flexible," and 1 percent "creative/entrepreneurial." Within the public sector: 75 percent were "controlling/hierarchical," 0 percent were "competitive/market-driven," 13 percent were "flexible/collaborative," and 13 percent were "creative/entrepreneurial." Private sector organizations reported having much greater variation in corporate culture, and relatively greater success with diversity management strategies.

Based upon the data, public sector organizations appeared to be less likely to have effective diversity management strategies, by virtue of being dominated by controlling/hierarchical cultures, and by having so little variation in corporate motivation. The complete absence of a competitive/market-driven culture was of particular interest.

Senior leader engagement

Hypothesis 4—Diversity management strategies are more effective in organizations with equitably engaged senior leadership.

Respondents were asked "To what extent are senior leaders engaged in diversity activities and informal discussions with stakeholders?" They were given an 11-point scale from which to choose their response, with 0 being the lowest level of engagement and 10 being the highest. There was a wide range of responses. Overall, senior leadership engagement was average. This data was then disaggregated in order to explore whether or not there was an optimal level of engagement in order to have an "effective" strategy.

Where diversity practitioners reported effectiveness of their diversity strategy was "effective," senior leadership engagement in informal discussions and activities was very varied. Where diversity practitioners reported effectiveness of their diversity management strategy was "somewhat effective," the level of senior leadership engagement in informal discussions and activities continued to be at an average level with a high degree of variation.

This global data was disaggregated according to private and public sector. The results showed slightly higher engagement of senior leaders within the private sector, as well as a much larger variance of leadership engagement in the public sector. This data was further disaggregated and analyzed according to effectiveness of diversity management strategies.

The global data was also cross-tabulated in order to compare the level of engagement of senior leaders with the dominant corporate motivation behind the diversity management strategy.

The overall level of engagement in organizations where motivation is primarily legal compliance is below average levels of senior management engagement (mean = 3.64). Organizations that were primarily driven by profit maximization showed a higher, yet average level of senior engagement (mean = 4.67). It appeared there is higher engagement and least variation when the main corporate motivation for a diversity management strategy is "moral responsibility" (mean = 6.00).

There was strong variation in organizations mainly motivated by "legal compliance" and "profit maximization." Those motivated by legal compliance demonstrated a much lower level of senior management engagement. Those motivated mainly by "profit maximization" showed slightly higher levels of engagement of senior leaders. Where moral responsibility was the key motivation, senior management engagement was highest. There were only two out of the 31 practitioners who responded in this way, which is a statistically insignificant number.

Organizational equity

> Hypothesis 5—Diversity management strategies are more effective where there is a high level of organizational equity.

Respondents were asked: "To what extent has your organization achieved organizational equity (operates fairly and transparency for all employees regardless of legally protected characteristics)?" Of the 31 responses, 15 percent said "low," 64 percent said "medium," and 21 percent said "high." The results show that a majority of organizations had an organizational culture in which organizational equity is on a "medium" level.

This data was then cross-tabulated against perceptions of how effective the overall diversity strategy is considered to be. These results show that when organizational equity is high the diversity management strategy is "somewhat effective" (mean = 2.67). As organizational equity decreases the effectiveness of diversity management strategy increases. The data show diversity management strategies are most effective when organizational equity is low, although here is much larger variation and standard deviation in diversity management performance within this category.

There is a little statistical difference between the different levels of organizational equity, which would lead one to believe its presence overall does not have much of an overall impact on the effectiveness of the diversity management strategy. Thus, the data does not support the hypothesis that higher organizational equity results in greater effectiveness of the diversity management strategy.

Organizational perception of diversity

> Hypothesis 6—Diversity management strategies are more effective when diversity is seen as an asset within an organization.

How diversity is perceived within an organization may have an impact upon the effectiveness of a diversity management strategy. If an organization is working from a deficit, compliance-based model, then it is likely diversity may be seen as something

that detracts value, or something that makes no difference at all. If a company is working from an asset model, then diversity management may be more likely to be seen as
something which adds value and which is a necessary license to operate.

Respondents were asked to complete this statement: "Thinking about the general
corporate climate, in your experience, diversity management within your organization
is seen primarily by stakeholders as…" They were given a choice between: "an impediment which detracts value," "a vital strategic resource which adds value," "a necessary license to operate," "something which makes no difference at all," and "other."
Respondents were able to choose as many categories as they felt were relevant to their
organization.

Eighteen percent of practitioners said diversity was seen as "an impediment which
detracts value," 61 percent of practitioners said diversity is seen as a "vital resource that
adds value," 13 percent said it was "a necessary requirement for a license to operate,"
9 percent said it is "something which makes no difference at all," and 12 percent said
"other" (people would like to be left alone, important but not vital given economic
crisis, an issue of political correctness when business is making money and something
which differs according to stakeholder). This data was cross-tabulated with the overall
effectiveness of diversity management strategies.

Where diversity management was "very effective" diversity was seen only as "a vital
strategic resource that adds value." There was only one respondent who fell into this
category. The data show a majority of respondents considered their diversity strategies
were "effective."

When diversity management is seen as "effective," 30 percent of practitioners see
diversity as "an impediment which detracts value," 70 percent said diversity is seen as "a
vital strategic resource that adds value," 10 percent said it was "a necessary requirement
to operate," and 10 percent said "other" (differs by stakeholder).

Where diversity management strategy was seen as "somewhat effective," 13 percent
said "diversity was an impediment," 47 percent said it was a "strategic resource," 53
percent said it was a "requirement to operate," 7 percent said it "made no difference
at all," and 13 percent said "other" (people to be left alone, important not vital given
economics). There was a large shift in perception regarding diversity management being
a "necessary license to operate." This increased significantly from "effective" to "somewhat effective" strategies.

Where diversity was "neither effective nor ineffective," 67 percent said "vital strategic resource," 33 percent said it was "a necessary license to operate," 33 percent said
it "makes no difference," 33 percent said "other" (an issue of political correctness that
is ok when business is making money). It is strong on "vital strategic resource," however, the perception of it being a necessary requirement and something which makes
no difference at all is significantly higher, in comparison to strategies where diversity
management is perceived as "effective."

For the remaining categories of "somewhat ineffective" and "very ineffective"
there was only one response for each category. Therefore, data is not strong enough
to draw any conclusion. Nonetheless, in the category of "somewhat ineffective"
diversity management strategy was said to be perceived as "a vital strategic resource,"
"a necessary requirement," and "something which makes no difference." In the "very
ineffective" category, diversity is seen as "an impediment" and "a necessary license
to operate."

This data was disaggregated to show whether or not there are any differences in perceptions between private and public sectors. The results show that in the private sector, 18 percent said it was "an impediment which detracts value," 68 percent of diversity practitioners said diversity is seen as "a vital strategic resource that adds value," 23 percent said it was "a necessary license to operate," 14 percent said it was "something which makes no difference at all," and 3 percent said "other" (important but not vital given economic crisis, differs according to stakeholders and political correctness when business is making money).

In the public sector, 25 percent said diversity was seen as "an impediment that detracts value," 25 percent said it was "a vital strategic resource," 75 percent said it was seen as "a necessary license to operate," 0 percent said "it is something that makes no difference at all."

Based upon the data, in the public sector diversity is seen as a much greater impediment, much less as a strategic resource, and something required in order to operate. There was a significant difference between sectors that suggested the public sector was engaging in diversity from the standpoint of "having no choice." No one from the public sector said diversity was seen as something that made no difference at all.

In-house diversity practitioners profile

There are potentially a large variety of frameworks, activities, priorities, and approaches to diversity management. It is possible that in-house diversity practitioners and their efforts may be too disparate to be of any greater impact. Toward the end of the questionnaire, in-house practitioners were asked to consider any similarities and differences that may exist between them as a group of practitioners. Their responses were open-ended. Content analysis was carried out on the responses in order to identify key themes, which are reported below.

Commonalities

The key themes that emerged, in order of prevalence, were as follows: passion; risk-taking/change agents; understanding of the business and the business case; knowledge; isolation/powerlessness; shared beliefs; and articulate and persuasive.

Passion was the most common characteristic of in-house diversity practitioners, which suggests they have a high amount of energy and commitment to their agenda. They also see themselves as change agents with a substantial amount of knowledge of their subject matter and of the businesses within which they function.

There were reports of feeling isolated and powerless within the organization, which echoed when reflect feedback I received as an external consultant from some in-house diversity and inclusion practitioners. This suggested the energy that in-house diversity practitioners bring into their organizations was not always fully utilized for the benefit of the social justice agenda. This presents itself as a real barrier to further progress and should be explored more fully.

Dissimilarities

When in-house diversity practitioners were asked if there were any key differences between them as practitioners, key themes which emerged were: none, conceptual framework (i.e. equality, diversity, or inclusion); board-level support; and organizational culture.

Qualitative responses to this question, and quantitative data within the questionnaire, suggest there was variation within the conceptual and operating frameworks of in-house diversity practitioners. Some remained driven by the legal case for diversity. This was particularly the case within the public sector. Others were driven primarily by profit maximization, fueled by the business case for diversity, supporting a valuing diversity paradigm in which diversity is seen as an asset. There was a very small percentage of practitioner organizations operating from the moral case for diversity. The question arose, "Why so few?"

Discussion

The In-House Diversity Practitioner Questionnaire provided an opportunity to compare and contrast corporate cultures on the dimension of public versus private sector experiences of in-house practitioners. This was an opportunity to explore whether or not private sector practitioners have comparable or divergent experiences of diversity management within their organizations. This discussion highlights points of similarity and dissimilarity between sectors.

Diversity management practices are more successful in the private sector

This questionnaire study explored whether or not there were a difference in diversity management effectiveness between sectors. The data suggests there is a difference between diversity management performances within the private sector and the public sector. Private sector in-house diversity practitioners reported having "effective" strategies, whereas public sector diversity practitioners reported "somewhat effective" strategies. In addition, there was much greater variation in diversity management performance within the public sector.

The business case and a distinct lack of moral fiber

Within diversity literature, three main cases for diversity are cited. They are legal, business case, and moral. Of these cases, those that appeared to predominate were legal and business. However, it was hypothesized that organizations driven by moral responsibility would have more effective diversity management strategies in place for the benefit of all stakeholders.

The data showed a very small portion of organizations driven by moral responsibility. Thirty percent of organizations were motivated by legal compliance, 36 percent of organizations were motivated by profit maximization, 27 percent were motivated by something "other," which was defined as: staff engagement, reputation management, service delivery, senior leadership support, creativity and compliance, talent shortages, research, and developing tools to help other companies. Only 6.45 percent (two respondents out of 31) said their organization was motivated primarily by a moral responsibility, which was a significantly low percentage.

Given these two responses in support of moral responsibility, the overall effectiveness of diversity strategy appears to go in the direction of "effective" to "very effective," with the two responses falling within these categories. However, because the percentage is so low, it was not possible to draw any firm conclusions about the impact of moral responsibility on diversity management strategy effectiveness. In order to either confirm, or disconfirm, the hypothesis that organizations motivated primarily by moral responsibility have diversity strategies that outperform those who do not, we need a larger number of morally driven organizations. This we do not have. The question of "Why not?" is a very interesting one worthy of further investigation. The fundamental questions could be: "Is it possible for organizations to be primarily morally driven?" "Does morality impede profitability?"

Thus, the question arose: "Why are there so few organizations motivated primarily by moral responsibility?" This is a particularly relevant question when data showed legal compliance alone does not yield improved social justice outcomes, and that the evidence for the business case for diversity is partially tenable. The data suggested that moral responsibility may have a positive impact upon overall corporate culture within which diversity strategies are being carried out.

The legal case for diversity, which dates back to the 1960s–1980s, proved to be ineffective. Consequently, having experienced very little substantive change, the business case for diversity was formulated in the 1990s. This provided human resource professionals with a language of finance that could be used to persuade senior managers, and in particular directors of finance, to invest money in developing multicultural organizations. Twenty years on, substantive changes have yet to be achieved, and even in some instances equality has regressed. It appears as though a shift in paradigm is required, and the case for moral responsibility might help to move things forward. We, as researchers and practitioners, may like to determine what the barriers are to accepting this case and consider establishing strategies to overcome these barriers.

When this data is broken down by sector, it reveals that the private sector is more motivated by profit maximization (50 percent) than it was by legal compliance (23 percent) and moral responsibility (9 percent). The public sector, on the other hand, was motivated primarily by legal compliance (88 percent) and by something "other," which was defined as self-audit (12 percent). It is important to note that none of the diversity practitioners representing the public sector cited their main corporate motivation was a moral responsibility. This is an unsettling revelation, given the civic duty of the public sector.

When corporate motivation was then cross-tabulated with effectiveness of the diversity management strategy, the data suggested that organizations motivated primarily by profit maximization tended to have "effective" diversity management performance. Whereas, organizations motivated by legal compliance tended to have "somewhat effective" diversity management performance overall, and will tend toward being more "ineffective."

If the public sector is and continues to be motivated primarily by legal compliance, then it greatly compromises its ability not only to be effective, but also to compete effectively with the private sector. It is also a concern that there is no consideration of profit maximization within the public sector.

Today the public sector within the United Kingdom, and in other Western European economies, is stretched and challenged financially, as a consequence of the current economic crisis. Governments and governmental institutions not only have to think about value for money, they have to think about how to make money. Civil servants have not been accustomed to being business people. Even if they were, the business case language around diversity is not part of their vernacular. Meanwhile, the business world has evolved toward the language of inclusion.

Not only does the public sector appear to lack diversity management language ground in business discourse, it appears to fundamentally lack moral imperative despite its central function and role within society. Based on the centrality of morality to public service, if the public sector does not, or has not yet, accepted a widespread moral responsibility for the equality, diversity, and inclusion agenda then what hope is there for diversity management within the public sector?

The data suggested that there may be greater hope for diversity management within the private sector, as this is the only sector in which respondents reported the dominant corporate motivation as being moral responsibility. It may just be that the private sector is more equipped to lead the way, as it is not as bogged down by legal mandates and imperatives as is the public sector.

"Other" motivations (which included membership expectation, staff engagement, external profile, improving service performance, customer satisfaction, combination of legal and profit, combination of creativity and compliance, and the development of research tools to provide support to companies) were all reported as being "somewhat effective." It may also be worth exploring these motivations further, in order to determine if there is any greater value embedded in them that have yet to be fully appreciated by practitioners.

Controlling hierarchies are more effective

> *Hypothesis 3—Diversity management strategies are more effective in flexible and collaborative organizational cultures.*

It was hypothesized that organizations with cultures that are predominately collaborative/flexible in nature would be better placed to support diversity management initiatives, than would be controlling/hierarchical, competitive/market-driven, creative/entrepreneurial, and other cultures.

When corporate cultures were then compared to overall effectiveness of diversity management strategy, results suggested that collaborative/flexible organizations yielded the most effective results. This supports the hypothesis that flexible/collaborative cultures will have more effective diversity management strategies. To the contrary, data show cultures are least effective in comparison to collaborative/flexible and competitive/market-driven cultures.

There appears to be a more complex dynamic at play. Public sector organizations are highly hierarchical. This would suggest they should underperform in comparison to private sector organizations overall in their diversity management. It may be that a lack of a competitive/market-driven approach may detract from effective diversity management within the public sector.

It is also arguable that, despite having strong controlling/hierarchical cultures, public sector organizations overall perform less well than private sector organizations due to the primary motivator being legal compliance, and to the absence of any motivation by moral responsibility.

Complexity theory purports that command and control and managerialism are not the most effective or equitable managerial approaches. The public sector is heavy on these forms of management, which may be why it is demonstrably worse at diversity management than the private sector. There is more variation in the private sector, most likely due to the fact that regulatory impositions are not so severely felt in the private sector as they are in the public sector.

Senior leadership engagement helps to improve effectiveness

> *Hypothesis 4—Diversity management strategies are more effective in organizations with equitably engaged senior leadership.*

It was hypothesized that the quality of leadership and engagement of senior leaders, in informal discussions and activities with stakeholders, would strengthen the effectiveness of a diversity management strategy. When diversity management strategies were considered to be "effective," there was an average level of engagement of senior leadership, and a substantial amount of variation between responses. When diversity practitioners reported effectiveness of their diversity management strategy was "somewhat effective," the level of senior leadership engagement had dropped slightly. Overall there was greater engagement of senior leaders within the private sector than in the public sector.

The results show highest levels of engagement are potentially found in organizations driven moral responsibility, although, as has already been discussed, the number of organizations falling within this category was not statistically significant enough.

Aside from moral responsibility, the highest and most statistically significant level of senior leader engagement was found when the main corporate motivation was profit maximization. The lowest level of senior leadership engagement was found when organizations are driven primarily by legal compliance.

Legal compliance as a main driver usually depends upon the command and control, the passing down of responsibilities within the organization to middle and lower management in order that organizations may "control" their employees behaviors and reduce risk of non-compliance. In such a circumstance, leaders may feel it is not their responsibility to "lead from the front" or "lead by their actions," hence the disconnection of senior level leaders from the core of the workforce.

The literature reviewed earlier discussed the importance of the relationship between the diversity climate and the ethical climate of an organization. It may be that such disconnection of the senior team may be seen as a low level of business ethics, particularly if senior people openly act in ways that contravene legislation and corporate policy and they themselves are not held to account.

Organizations don't have to be equitable in order to be effective

> *Hypothesis 5—Diversity management can be effective even when organizations are not equitable*

A majority of organizations had an organizational culture in which organizational equity is on a "medium" level. When this data was then cross-tabulated against perceptions of how effective the overall diversity strategy is considered to be, it showed diversity management strategies are most effective when organization equity is "low." This result is somewhat confusing.

A low level of organizational equity is the only condition in which any diversity management strategy was considered to be "very ineffective." This result does not support the hypothesis.

The diversity management strategy was more effective, the higher the organizational equity. The data show diversity management strategies are least effective when organizational equity is high, which is the exact opposite outcome anticipated.

This is also an unexpected result, particularly in the private sector, where most diversity practitioners report their strategies are "effective" in creating fairer outcomes for all and inclusive work environments. It presents the question: "How does an organization achieve equity for all (inclusion) in conditions in which organizational equity is considered to be low and the diversity management strategy is considered to be 'effective'? What is the diversity management strategy actually 'achieving'?" The data cannot answer this question, though it is an interesting question to explore further. This study looked at the "perception" of diversity management effectiveness; however, it did not identify key objective measures to establish such effectiveness.

Earlier data also posed the question of "How can an organization have achieved equity for all (regardless of social groupings) if the same organizations have achieved average and below average results for a majority of the nine legally protected characteristics?" It was suggested there is a division between equity for an individual (valuing diversity) and equity for a social group (equality of opportunity). Is it easier to achieve the latter than the former? An explanation for diversity management being seen as effective when equity is low may be because social equity remains low while personal equity, and a focus upon the individual, remains a high priority.

A low level of equity suggests there is not a fair distribution of power and influence within an organization. Another explanation may be perhaps this perception drives people to realize the value of diversity, not only for minorities, but also for people who are perceived to be part of the majority.

Another possibility, which may cause more concern than other explanations, is that practitioners may define diversity management strategies as being "effective" and "somewhat effective" despite organizational equity not having been achieved and pointing to the contrary being true about the effectiveness of diversity management strategies. What this study does not provide are exact metrics upon which effectiveness is based. This is an age-old dilemma within diversity, finding concrete metrics upon which to measure performance.

Diversity has to be appreciated as a vital strategic resource

Hypothesis 6—Diversity management strategies are more effective when diversity is seen as an asset within an organization.

The data supported the hypothesis when diversity is perceived as "a vital strategic resource which adds value" throughout an organization, then diversity management strategies will be more effective than in organizations which do not perceive diversity in this way. Overall more respondents said that diversity was seen within their organization as a "vital strategic resource that adds value" (61 percent), 18 percent of practitioners said diversity was seen as "an impediment which detracts value," 13 percent said it was "a necessary requirement for a license to operate," 9 percent said it is "something which makes no difference at all," and 12 percent said "other" (people would like to be left alone, important but not vital given economic crisis, an issue of political correctness when business is making money and something which differs according to stakeholder).

When overall effectiveness of diversity management strategies was mapped against these responses, data showed that organizations with a strong sense of there being such value had "effective" diversity management strategies (70 percent). Where diversity management strategies were seen to be "somewhat effective," the overriding perception of diversity within a culture is a diversity management strategy it was "a necessary license to operate" (53 percent). Even when diversity management is seen as "neither effective nor ineffective" the strongest perception of diversity it was "a vital strategic resource which adds value" (67 percent).

When overall perceptions were disaggregated by sector, data showed that within the private sector the main perception of diversity was it is "a vital strategic resource which adds value" (68 percent), and in the public sector the main perception of diversity was "it is a necessary license in order to operate" (75 percent). This data was consistent with Hypothesis 1, which argued that private sector performance was stronger than public sector performance. The perception of the value of diversity appeared to have an influence upon this sector-based difference.

This was a significant difference between sectors, suggesting the public sector was engaging in diversity from the standpoint of "having no choice." No one from the public sector said diversity was seen as something that makes no difference at all. It may be public sector performance is suffering due to the perception diversity management as something that "has to be done"; it is an imposition created by its own legislative mandates.

The data showed that diversity was seldom seen as "a vital strategic resource which adds value" within the public sector. As a sector, the public sector appeared to be focused upon its need to always show "value for money." If the sector tends to see no intrinsic value in diversity, then it stands to reason that fewer resources will be dedicated to diversity management strategies. For instance, when exploring the effectiveness of various diversity activities in a previous section, private sector activity which is most effective is "staffing and infrastructure" at top of the list as most "effective" activity. It was somewhere in the middle within the public sector.

This suggests there may be a certain level of structure, stability, and investment in diversity management strategies, within the private sector, which enables better results to be achieved. It is argued that diversity management practice within the public sector will continue to be weak should the sector continue to fail to see and understand the strategic value of diversity. Data show that the public sector is still operating according to an equalities framework, primarily driven by legal compliance, a hierarchical/controlling management structure, which engages very little with other stakeholders.

Data suggests organizations that are controlling/hierarchical cultures, with a competitive/market-driven culture focused upon profit maximization, with moderate levels of informal senior leadership engagement and low levels of organizational equity, are those with "effective" diversity management strategies.

The risk of diversity and inclusion professionals burning out

Key themes that emerged were, in order to prevalence, as follows: passion; risk-takers/ change agents; understanding of the business and the business case; knowledge; isolation/powerlessness; shared beliefs; and articulate and persuasive. The most common characteristic identified was passion.

The data suggest in-house diversity practitioners are, by and large, a group of individuals who are firmly committed to, and passionate about, issues of social justice. They have high levels of energy, strength of will, and determination to see through organizational change. It would be ideal if this level of intensity would be matched by seeing a greater number of effective and very effective diversity management strategies. Yet, practitioners by and large reported that diversity management strategies were on the lower end of "effective," bordering "somewhat effective." This outcome may be the cause of "frustration" in-house diversity practitioners, which they identified themselves as experiencing.

Potentially key detractors were cited as: "isolation and powerlessness within the organization," "frustration with limited agenda," and "lack of leadership." If in-house diversity practitioners are experiencing isolation and powerlessness within their organizations then it makes it difficult to translate their energy, commitment, and professionalism into organizational practice. Isolation is a major barrier and may also be an indication of an organization neither understanding, nor fully embracing the value of diversity. In such a circumstance, it may be likely that in-house diversity practitioners feel as though they are simply "box-ticking," and assisting in an organization's need to demonstrate legal compliance.

"Frustration with the limited agenda" may stem from the fact that organizations have varying approaches to the social justice agenda. Some are focused upon equality-based issues. Some are focused upon valuing diversity. Some are motivated by equity for all (inclusion). These may be key variables that have an impact upon the effectiveness of an overall diversity management strategy, as well as on the effectiveness of in-house diversity practitioners. It is worth future research exploring these variables in more detail.

Dissimilarities

In-house diversity practitioners were also asked if there were any key differences between them as practitioners. The key themes that emerged from a content analysis were: none, conceptual framework (i.e. equality, diversity, or inclusion), board-level support, and organizational culture.

The theme referred to most often as dissimilarity is the focus of the framework within which diversity practitioners are operating. Data suggest a fair amount of variation exists between practitioners who take an equalities approach, a diversity approach, and an inclusion approach. Several practitioners report feeling frustrated by a purely equalities approach to social justice and by the lack of focus upon inclusion. They appear to argue in favor of inclusion frameworks being more effective in order to build and to execute diversity management strategies.

The other factors mentioned by in-house diversity practitioners are board-level engagement and the organizational cultures within which in-house diversity practitioners operate. Other data within this research show even within organizations in which diversity management is seen to be "effective," the level of engagement is very low.

Data generated from this questionnaire study also highlights the relationship between the organizational culture and diversity management strategy effectiveness. It appears collaborative/flexible cultures are currently performing better than controlling/hierarchical and competitive/market-driven cultures. The key differences can be identified as relating to: the sector within which one is operating (with the private sector performing better as evidenced in the data); an equality approach versus an inclusive approach (with the private sector demonstrating stronger performance with equity for all); agency of diversity practitioner; levels of staffing and resourcing; and board-level engagement. Despite there being some key differences, overall, in-house diversity practitioners believed there were more similarities between themselves than dissimilarities.

A majority of practitioners believe diversity strategies employed by their organizations are either "effective" or "somewhat effective." Data supports the supposition made by previous research that diversity management practices are not very effective. With such average results, data suggests there are certain barriers to progress that have yet been identified as part of overall diversity management strategy.

Where there is variation, there appear to be only single responses in three of those categories: "very effective," "somewhat ineffective," and "very ineffective." Three respondents said "somewhat ineffective." This variation demonstrates the possibility of different diversity management outcomes on the dimension of effectiveness, however, the number of respondents is too small and no conclusion can be drawn from it.

With one respondent who reported having a "very effective" strategy, one can look at other conditions of this respondent's organization to see if those conditions support the main hypotheses of this book. Again, since the sample size is so small, data is not robust enough to support the main hypotheses.

Lip service and box-ticking are both far too prevalent; practitioners should be very wary of committing their passion, their time, and energy to organizations that have no real desire or capability of transforming their cultures in order to be more fair, equitable, and just. Diversity practitioners may be at risk of being co-opted into the very status quo they wish to improve. The achievement of Rule of Law within diversity management, in which fundamental human rights, and dignity and respect for the individual are upheld, has yet to be fully embraced.

Even where there is well-defined moral responsibility within an organization, diversity management cannot succeed in the absence of financial investment in diversity infrastructure, which includes staffing and resourcing, as well as capital expenditure to support business activities and initiatives. In order to gain access to finances, we as diversity practitioners have been caught in a deceptive web of an unproved and untenable business case for diversity. Pressing diversity practitioners to justify financially the legitimacy of diversity management is a large part of the process of co-opting diversity management into the status quo of predatory capitalism. There is an unresolved conflict of values here that needs further redress.

Limitations

The sample size of 31 respondents is small. Therefore, it is difficult to generalize from the results. Data provides a good baseline of information upon which further investigations and research can be conducted.

Another key limitation of this study is the data is based upon subjective opinions and experiences of in-house diversity practitioners. No hard metrics were used in the questionnaire in order to substantiate their perspectives.

A technical concern is the different point scales used to capture perceptions of the overall effectiveness of the diversity management strategy and the point scale used to consider strand-specific diversity management performance. The former has a 7-point scale and the latter a 6-point scale. If this research is replicated then the same scale would need to be used across the whole of the questionnaire where comparisons are to be made.

Future research directions

Any researchers who wish to replicate this survey should seek to increase the number of respondents in order to confirm or disconfirm the validity of the data and conclusions drawn from it.

Other issues, generated by this data, which can be explored within the context of this questionnaire study, or as independent studies, include the following: whether or not public sector performance can be improved by introducing elements of private sector culture and orientation to diversity; why moral responsibility is so weak as a dominant corporate motivation; why progress in certain areas of equality (i.e. sexual orientation, and race) is weaker than in others (i.e. gender, equity for all, and pregnancy/maternity); and last, if a reduction in investment in diversity initiatives has any effect on the overall effectiveness of a diversity management strategy.

Respondents in this questionnaire survey were primarily from the United Kingdom, with a small sample from Europe. Future research should also seek to engage in-house diversity practitioners within other economic regions. Borrowing ideas from Hofstede (1980), and his cultural dimension, it would be particularly interesting if future research were to generate data of countries/organizations which are, for instance, strongly hierarchical while at the same time as being very collective in orientation and compare to compare this with countries/organizations which tend to be more flexible/collaborative and individualistic in orientation.

Such data would enable us to explore if wider cultural contexts within which businesses operate have significant influence on the overall effectiveness of a diversity management strategy, and what optimal conditions for high performance may be. The financial world is turning its attention more toward emerging markets in order to find exit routes out of current economic decline. Therefore, determining the extent to which traditional diversity strategies (designed according to Anglo-Saxon values) are at all relevant within these cultural contexts of emerging markets is of particular importance.

12 Embracing an Ethical Performance Improvement Campaign (EPIC) Journey

> If the impulse to daring and bravery is too fierce and violent, stay it with guidance and instruction.
>
> —Xun Zi

Researchers have called for a more nuanced approach to effective diversity management, and have challenged researchers and practitioners to address the inherent power struggles that exist within organizations, and to ask the difficult questions about the impact that these power struggles have on diversity management. In answer to this call, and in moving the diversity management agenda forward, I have taken a deep, close look at organizational and leadership ethics, and married ethics to diversity management practice. Years of practical and research experience have led me to believe that ethical, engaged, and enlightened executive leadership is at the core of successful diversity management strategy. Experience has also taught me that governance structure and long-term strategy are also at the heart of diversity management success. In pulling theory and practice together, this is how I came to formulate and call the Ethical Performance Improvement Campaign (EPIC) Journey, a strategic methodology aimed at enhancing diversity and improving social justice outcomes.

The EPIC Journey highlights the importance of an ethical organizational climate, and the ability to address power relations within an organization, in relation to effective diversity management. It presents a data driven, long-term, in-depth methodology to improve the diversity management performance of organizations. It is modeled around research literature in the fields of diversity management, organizational equity, stakeholder engagement, complexity theory, business ethics, corporate responsibility, and moral leadership. It is designed to help researchers and practitioners collect a wide array of data, from which they can establish developmental targets, build strategies, and define appropriate initiatives to help reach those targets. Robust performance data is generated so that the impact of diversity management initiatives upon the business, teams, and individuals is measurable, tangible, and demonstrable.

First and foremost, the campaign is focused upon strengthening the ethics of an organization, and creates the opportunity for diversity experts to share their expert knowledge directly with senior executives who are the key powerbrokers within organizations. This, in turn, enables executive leaders to work collaboratively, seamlessly, and credibly, with other key stakeholders, including diversity and inclusion professionals.

The Ethical Performance Improvement Campaign requires senior executives to make serious personal commitments to social change and social justice, and to allow for a level of social activism within themselves, their employees, and their organization, that has the potential of challenging, and even of destabilizing, status quos. Technically, that phrase means discriminating between those who are competent from those who are less competent. It is a call to action for senior executives and leaders to really step up to the plate, and to engage in ways that acknowledge their knowledge gaps, their ignorance, their insecurities, and most of all their humanity. There are several things that can be achieved with this EPIC Journey, and which are outlined in this chapter.

EPIC Journey benefits

The EPIC Journey promotes an inclusive framework that integrates and balances equality, diversity, and inclusion frameworks

The EPIC Journey provides a fully-formed holistic approach to diversity management. With structured governance at its core, the EPIC Journey's framework balances out the needs of all individuals and groups, while at the same time, addresses the unique circumstances of those for whom equity and social justice have not been achieved.

Discomfort with differences continues to affect people's ability to speak openly and freely about these differences and about how they can be of enormous benefit. In such a circumstance, it is difficult to value and to respect diversity. If this is not possible, then it is also not possible to create inclusive cultures. The challenge of executive leadership is to help people to unpick and debunk false notions of equality, diversity, and inclusion, and to understand strategically and systematically how to utilize and apply the concepts of equality, diversity, and inclusion.

Senior executives and leaders are clear in their minds as to what the differences are between equality, diversity, and inclusion. With this clarity, they lead on and take full ownership of the diversity management agenda. This ownership makes it easier to achieve long-term, sustainable improvements in social justice outcomes through diversity management.

Increases senior executives' diversity confidence, engagement, and credibility

Senior executive leadership is a key ingredient to diversity management success. The EPIC Journey starts with a top-down process that works closely with senior executives and leaders, by giving them the time, attention, and support they require to find their confidence and their credibility as diversity champions. It does this by an expert diversity and inclusion practitioner, either internal or external to an organization, providing one-to-one coaching to senior executives. Senior executives are given a safe space to voice their concerns and to begin to build a better understanding of the complexities of equality, diversity, and inclusion, and of how to live up to the leadership expectations and responsibilities they already possess within their organizations.

Most importantly, these sessions explore how equality, diversity, and inclusion are relevant for successful business performance within the key business area, or areas, for which a senior executive is responsible. This is an essential dialog that removes diversity management from the financial periphery of senior executives, and places it squarely within the context of a senior executive's day-to-day leadership responsibilities.

This helps to ground senior executives, and gives them a language, and an understandable business construct, that helps them to understand and communicate their responsibilities from a position of clarity. It also prepares them to be challenged openly and honestly, and to allow for the disruption of status quos, while at the same time they can maintain and strengthen their authority. They become true diversity champions. The EPIC Journey enables them to step up to the plate, and to engage as fully-fledged members of the organizational team, and as integral parts of the whole.

It is important that these leaders are coached and up-skilled so that their diversity champion position is a substantive one. When those in positional power cannot develop the skills of a diversity virtuoso, then they should prepare to share their positional power with those who do have the skills, in order to enable real diversity experts to effect change.

Liberates the diversity and inclusion function from human resources

Traditionally, diversity professionals have been situated within human resources and have been labeled as the "conscience of an organization." The EPIC Journey changes this dynamic, by encouraging and supporting senior executives to take on the role of "the organizational conscience." By doing so, they embrace a new level of moral leadership, enabling them to lead by example, and thus helping them to avoid criticism and a perceived lack of credibility.

Human resource management is an integral part of the Diversity Quality Cycle of governance, but it is only a small part. By taking a business–centric approach to diversity management, it is clear that the responsibility of the agenda lies in all areas of the business. This takes the focus off Human Resources, and creates a forum for discussions to take place regarding the impact of equality, diversity, and inclusion across business functions.

Increases employee engagement through participative and democratic governance

Central to the EPIC Journey is the Diversity Quality Cycle, a model of participative governance that touches all stakeholders, vertically and horizontally, and all aspects of an organization's core business functions. In this cycle, senior executives and leaders are active members of the diversity and inclusion governance structure, along with other selected employees and external stakeholders. If it is not practical for all senior executives to sit on such a committee, then they make a strategic decision as to which senior executives occupy seats on the Diversity & Inclusion Committee, and for how long. The view is to have a healthy rotation over time so that all executives are engaged.

The EPIC Journey gives senior executives a roadmap and guidance to better engagement, and in turn inspire other employees to engage more fully with the diversity management agenda. The Diversity Quality Cycle, as part of the EPIC Journey, can help to restore lost faith when senior executives are seen to be coming out of their shells. As a governance model, it helps to keep executive power in check and balance, thus creating a more democratic ethos within the organizational culture. This in turn, can be helpful in increasing people's sense of empowerment and worth.

What is also important about the Diversity Quality Cycle is that it allows for productive social activism within an organization; creates a spirit of collaboration; creates a social fabric that helps to make organizational cultures more cohesive; and gives people an opportunity to engage in meaningful work that reflects their personal valuing of and commitments to diversity and social justice. In short, it brings the diversity and inclusion agenda more to life.

The Diversity Quality Cycle is instrumental in facilitating a process of substantial shifts in the social justice outcomes within organizations. In addition, it provides a diversity management framework through which improvements in ethical decision-making can be achieved. The Diversity Quality Cycle provides a mechanism for capturing and for acting upon the views and opinions of a diverse and representative body of stakeholders in order to create improved diversity management outcomes.

The Diversity Quality Cycle is a tool that may be used beyond the purposes of traditional diversity management. While my main focus has been upon diversity management practices, the Diversity Quality Cycle, as a system of innovative and egalitarian governance, can and should be used as a framework for cultural transformations of any type, regardless of the subject matter. For instance, it could be used for change management around health and safety, customer support, or even the introduction and integration of new technologies within a business.

The Diversity Quality Cycle provides a framework designed to capture a diversity of stakeholder opinions and perspectives, and to integrate this information into decision-making processes of a given organization. Thus, it is envisaged, by applying the Diversity Quality Cycle, ethical and egalitarian decision-making can be significantly improved and as a result so too can social justice performance.

Generates robust data that measures demographic diversity, ethical climates, and business performance

Research has shown that data revealing the ethical climate of an organization should be considered closely within the context of diversity management, not just demographic data. While demographic data continues to be of the utmost importance in an organization's ability to track progress, it cannot stand alone. Very often the phrase, "walking the walk" is used regarding diversity management. In many instances, there is a disconnection between organizational rhetoric and organizational behavior. In such instances, organizations are not see as "walking the walk," and as falling short of being honest and transparent in their commitment to diversity and social justice.

The objective of the EPIC Journey is to create stronger values-based organizations that live the principles they espouse. If there is a disconnection between these principles and organizational behavior then this creates an internal tension. This, in turn, can slow down efforts to create more diverse, more equitable, and just working environments.

The EPIC Journey applies management science to diversity performance, and takes data collection beyond the surface of demographic data, and delves deeper into the ethical climates of organizations, and into institutional barriers that could be blocking diversity management progress. It helps organizations identify which areas of their ethical performance may be weak in relation to valuing diversity. Based upon this data, it is then possible to devise strategies to address any imbalances identified. The data helps to determine if perceived concerns are actually true concerns.

Navigating through diversity management using a moral compass

Diversity management is not just about demographics and numbers. It is about fairness and justice; morality underpins it. Managing diversity, the complexity of human relationships, and how this plays out in business, is a very difficult exercise, requiring highly skilled leadership.

Traditionally, diversity management has been led by an Anglo-American model, focused upon changing demographics and providing diversity training for staff. It is clear from global data that the United States of America's social justice and Rule of Law performance are just above average when it comes to it being seen as an egalitarian culture. Scandinavian and Northern European cultures rate most highly on the Social Justice and Rule of Law indices. There are many positive lessons to learn from the organization of Nordic countries, and their systems of governance.

Dismantling Diversity Management has delved into a wider body of academic research to explore which theories could add value to our pursuit of more effective diversity management, and improved social justice outcomes. It has taken a broader and longer view of what knowledge needs to be integrated into a contemporary model of diversity management. To this end, *Dismantling Diversity Management* has encouraged a greater appreciation for the complexity of the diversity management agenda, so that we can see beyond simple demographics, and more closely into the power dynamics and social justice within organizations.

It has presented and explained the function of the Diversity Quality Cycle, a model of collective engagement and governance that puts the value of diversity at its very core, and which operates according to democratic principles. It is sculpted around Nordic frameworks of justice and democracy, with a view to creating better social justice outcomes for diversity management. Diversity management, in the absence of democratic governance structures, will continue to make improving social justice outcomes merely aspirational.

It has placed executive and senior leaders at the helm of diversity management endeavors, and has presented a call to action to them to become true diversity champions, and not simply figureheads for a cause of which they may know very little about. As leaders of organizations they have to be seen to be doing more than just "being seen to be doing something." They have to do it, otherwise credibility and hope is lost, as is the cause. The action research study showed the detrimental impact on a disengaged leadership, and the unsustainability of the positive things that arose from the Diversity Quality Cycle.

As a research exercise in social justice, it was a very rewarding exercise for those who were involved. Their engagement and participation, as diversity champions, created a space for organizational equity, gave them a great sense of purpose, and an opportunity to strategically and structurally live out their values of equality, diversity, and inclusion. This was the case for all co-researchers and participants, bar the executive leadership team who kept greater than arms length away from personally engaging with the diversity management agenda.

Diversity champions, however, can go but so far, as a consequence of some of the institutional barriers that prevent them from having the voice and agency required in order for them to effect change. They have the skills, but often not the power. If their energy is not to be usurped, if diversity management is going to be effective, then they are very much reliant upon executive and senior leadership, those with the power, also exemplifying moral leadership.

The questionnaire that explored organizational conditions for effective diversity management, from the perspective of diversity and inclusion professionals, was helpful in shedding more light on the hypotheses that arose from the action research case study. It revealed that organizations motivated by a business case for diversity were more effective in their diversity management efforts than organizations that were primarily motivated by legal compliance.

In addition, the data twenty-first-century showed that public sector organizations were heavily motivated by legal compliance, and had very little discourse around or understanding of a business case for diversity for their organizations. Command and control management was the dominant style of organizational management in such instance, a style that is outdated given the demands of the twenty-first-century workplace. The diversity management performance appears to be weakest in the public sector.

What is most shocking is that there were so few organizations that say their primary motivation was a moral case for diversity. However, where this is the case, the data showed that these were the most effective organizations when it came to diversity management. With growing evidence about the importance of values-driven leadership, avoiding conversations about morality, and its place within business, is certainly part of the old-style diversity management practice that has to be questioned, and stopped.

The moral case for diversity is often overshadowed by both the business case and the legal case for managing diversity. Historically, the moral case has not carried the same degree of business legitimacy as the other two cases. Yet, diversity management practices have been marginally effective in the absence of the moral case for diversity. With more fully accepted and developed sense of business ethics and morality, it is possible to improve diversity management, and most importantly, social justice outcomes.

Clarity of the equality, diversity, and inclusion agendas, and engagement at all levels of an organization are required for effective diversity management. For the next generation of diversity management practice to succeed, it will require leadership courage, honesty, transparency, passion, integrity, and servitude. It will require greater moral leadership, balanced out with leadership that continues to be the financial and legal stewards of their organizations. The time is now for organizations to actively begin to dismantle their diversity management practices, and to examine critically the power relationships within their organizations. Organizations need to keep themselves in check, and to ensure that the way they have constructed their diversity management practice is not reinforcing the very status quos that diversity management is designed to challenge and to overcome.

Returning to the possibility that this book may just be my diversity management swan song, it appears to me that not all organizational cultures are driven by ethical leadership or designed to enhance diversity and embrace inclusion. It would be wonderful if it were universally possible for all organizations to embrace an EPIC Journey, and go the distance of substantially improving social justice outcomes, however, I do not believe this is realistic. It is very difficult to transform organizations that have deeply institutionalized discriminatory and other unethical practices and procedures that have endured over long periods of time. No matter how much these institutions tout their valuing of diversity and inclusion, what it takes to actually achieve such an organizational state, in reality, often runs counter to the organizational cultural ethos that may center around strong notions of compliance, competition, predatory capitalism, power dominance, short-termism, primary profit motivations, and legitimized unethical leadership. These organizations are often thought of as being "too big to fail." Within the context of diversity and inclusion, these very same organizations should be deemed to be too big to succeed. There is some organizational soul-searching to be done, which is all too often avoided or glossed over.

Looking to the future of diversity and inclusion, personally, I would like to see more investment made in working with SMEs that already have senior ethical, engaged, and enlightened leadership in existence. We are at a crucial, pivotal moment in history, a moment that is bearing the fruit of weak business ethics that have endured over time, weak ethics that leaders have attempted to cloak in media spin and corporate rhetoric. This is corporate and organizational irresponsibility, which despite investment in diversity management, continues to breed a sense of divisiveness, competition, and tensions between groups.

The health of our economies and our societies is dependent upon chief executive officers who are enlightened and engaged and who, most importantly, bring to their organizations the entrepreneurial spirit required to break new ground, to be true pioneers in challenging themselves, their systems, their organizations, and in challenging the societies in which we are living. We need more courageous executive leaders who are well versed in the balanced relationship between people, profit, and planet, to show willing to be trailblazers and risk-takers in their sectors and fields.

Having said that, we need these leaders to ignite within us all a sense of trust, faith, and empowerment, and a belief that our voices are legitimate, and that we have the power and the ability to influence to the good our organizations and our communities where we see and feel and know that things are not as they should be.

We all need to make some hard decisions about our own sense of wellbeing and belonging to the organizations and societies within which we work and live. We must all work together proactively, despite, and in light of, our perceived differences, in order to address the discrepancies and the injustices that we see occurring in our places of work and within society as a whole. We all, not just senior executive leaders, need to be and to act as leaders. If we say that we value diversity, inclusion, equity, fairness, dignity, respect, and wellbeing, then we all need to take responsibility for truly standing behind these values that we say we espouse, especially in the face of what we may perceive as opposition. How we face this "opposition" is the best test of the integrity of our own moral fiber. Life and business are not a zero sum games, where one side loses and one side wins. Above all else, we need more courageous visionaries and more critical and strategic thinkers to help renew and instill a sense of safety, hope, belonging, and prosperity.

The generation is at the beginning of its journey of taking over our societal helms. What we baby boomers and Generation Xs have provided them with is a form of diversity management that is negligent, deceiving, and defunct. It has been my ambition to dismantle diversity management now, for the benefit of the millennial generation, to say that we have gotten some things right over the years, but that we have continued to get many things wrong. It is understood that millennials are driven by purpose and not by profit. It may be a difficult concept for those of us who have come before them to understand, yet, the reality is, there are plenty of millennials who are occupying the bodies of baby-boomers and generation xs. It seems as though a critical mass of young people has come back full swing, to remind us, the aging population, of what values and ethics inspired us, back in our day, to do the work that we have been doing all these years, sometimes to no avail. I fundamentally believe that there is hope for the future, and that there is extreme power in inter-generational dialog and action. We just have to be prepared to relinquish and share our power and authority, to hand the reins over to our next generation of heirs. The journey continues.

References

Agrast, M.D., Botero, J.C., and Ponce, A. (2011).*The World Justice Project Rule of Law® 2011.* Washington: World Justice Project.

Amagoh, F. (2008). "Perspectives on Organizational Change: Systems and Complexity Theories." *The Innovation Journal: The Public Sector Innovation Journal*, 13(3), 1–14.

Anand, R. and Winters, M.F. (2008). "A Retrospective View of Corporate Diversity Training from 1964 to Present." *Academy of Management Learning and Education*, 7(3), 356–372.

Ashforth, B.E. and Gibbs, B.W. (1990). "The Double-Edge of Organizational Legitimation." *Organizational Science,* 1(5), 177–194.

Avis, J. (2009). "Further Education in England: The New Localism, Systems Theory and Governance." *Journal of Education Policy*, 24(5), 633–648.

Barktus, B.R. and Glassman, M. (2008). "Do Firms Practice What They Preach?" *Journal of Business Ethics*, 83(2), 207–216.

Bass, B.M. (1985). *Leadership and Performance beyond Expectations.* New York: Macmillan.

Bassett-Jones, N., Brown, R.B., and Cornelius, N. (2007). "Delivering Effective Diversity Management through Effective Structures." *Systems Research and Behavioral Science*, 24(1), 59–67.

Blackmore, J. (2006). "Deconstructing Diversity Discourses in the Field of Educational Management and Leadership." *Educational Management Administration & Leadership*, 34(2), 181–199.

Blasco, M. and Zølner, M. (2010). "Corporate Social Responsibility in Mexico and France: Exploring the Role of Normative Institutions". *Business & Society*, 49(2), 216–251.

Boswell, J. (1997). "Under-Development of Business Ethics." *Ethical Perspectives*, 4(2), 105–116.

Bowen, H. (1953). *Social Responsibilities of the Businessman.* New York: Harper & Row.

Brønn, P.S. and Vrioni, A.B. (2001). "Corporate Social Responsibility and Cause-Related Marketing: An Overview." *International Journal of Advertising*, 20(2), 207–222.

Carr, W. and Kemmis, S. (1986). *Becoming Critical: Education, Knowledge and Action Research.* New York: RoutledgeFarmer.

Carroll, A.B. (1999). "Corporate Social Responsibility: Evolution of a Definitional Construct." *Business in Society*, 38(3), 268–295.

Curtis, E.F. and Dreachslin, J. (2008). "Integrative Literature Review: DM Interventions and Organisational Performance: A Synthesis of Current Literature." *Human Resource Development Review*, 7(1), 107–134.

Dreachslin, J.L., Weech-Maldonao, R., and Dansky, K.H. (2004). "Racial and Ethnic Diversity and Organizational Behaviour: A Focused Research Agenda for Health Services Management." *Social Science & Medicine,* 59(5), 961–971.

Eden, C. and Huxham, C. (1996). "Action Research for Management Research." *British Journal of Management*, 7(1), 75–86.

Eilbert, H. and Parker, I.R. (1973). "The Current Status of Corporate Social Responsibility." *Business Horizons*, 16(2), 5–14.

Ely, R.J. (2004). "A Field Study of Group Diversity, Participation in Diversity Education Programs and Performance." *Journal of Organizational Behavior*, 25(6), 755–780.

Freeman, R.E. (1984). *Strategic Management: A Stakeholder Approach*. Boston: Pitman.

Griffin, R.W. (1988). "Consequences of Quality Circles in an Industrial: A Longitudinal Assessment." *Academy of Management Journal*, 31(2), 338–358.

Gustavsen, B. (1996). "Action Research, Democratic Dialogue, and the Issue of 'Critical Mass' in Change." *Qualitative Inquiry*, 2(1), 90–103.

Habermas, J. (1970). "Technology and Science as Ideology." *Toward a Rational Society*, 81(122), 107.

Hansen, F. (2003). "Diversity's Business Case Doesn't Add Up." *Workforce*, 82(4), 28–32.

Hargreaves, D. (2003). *Education Epidemic: Transforming Secondary Schools through Innovative Networks*. London: Demos.

Hartmann, T., Gao, J. and Fischer, M. (2008). "Areas of Application for 3D and 4D Models on Construction Projects." *Journal of Construction Engineering and management*, 134(10), 776–785.

Haseman, B. (2006). "A Manifesto for Performative Research." *Media International Australia incorporating Culture and Policy*, Theme Issue "Practice-led Research" (118), 98–106.

Herbig, P. and Milewicz, J. (1995). "The Relationship of Reputation and Credibility for Brand Success." *Journal of Consumer Marketing*, 12(4), 5–10.

Hofstede, G. (1980). "Motivation, Leadership, and Organization: Do American Theories Apply Abroad?" *Organizational Dynamics*, 9(1), 42–63.

Janssens, M. and Zanoni, P. (2005). "Many Diversities for Many Services: Theorizing Diversity (Management) in Service Companies." *Human Relations*, 58(3), 310–340.

Jayne, M.E.A. and Dipboye, R.L. (2004). "Leveraging Diversity to Improve Business Performance." *Human Resource Management*, 43(4), 409–424.

Johnston, W. and Packer, A. (1987). *Workforce 2000*. New York: Hudson Institute.

Jones, T.M. (1995). "Instrumental Stakeholder Theory: A Synthesis of Ethics and Economics." *Academy of Management Review*, 20(2), 404–437.

Kersten, A. (2000). "Diversity Management: Dialogue, Dialectics and Diversion." *Journal of Organizational Change Management*, 13(3), 235–248.

Kochan, T., Bezrukova, K., Ely, R., Jackson, S., Joshi, A., Jehn, K., Leonard, J., Levine, D., and Thomas, D. (2003). "The Effects of Diversity on Business Performance: Report of the Diversity Research Network." *Human Resource Management*, 42(1), 3–21.

Kossek, E., Markel, K.S., and McHugh, P.P. (2003). "Increasing Diversity as an HRM Change Strategy." *Journal of Organizational Change Management*, 16(3), 328–352.

Lewin, K. (1946). "Action Research and Minority Problems." *Journal of Social Issues*, 2(4), 34–46.

Lockwood, N.R. (2007). "Leveraging Employee Engagement for Competitive Advantage: HR's Strategic Role." *SHRM Quarterly*, 52(3), 1–11.

Lumby, J., Harris, A., Morrison, M., Muijs, D., Sood, K., Glover, D., Wilson, M., with Briggs, A. and Middlewood, D. (2005). *Leadership Development and Diversity in the Learning and Skills Sector*. London: LSDA.

Mackay, F. and Bilton, K. (2000). "Learning from Experience: Lessons in Mainstreaming Equal Opportunities." Edinburgh: Governance of Scotland Forum, University of Edinburgh.

Maldonado, N. and Lacey, C.H (2001). "Defining Moral Leadership: Perspectives of 12 Leaders." *Florida Journal of Educational Research*, Fall 2001, 41(1), 79–101.

Mason, R. (2007). "The External Environment's Effect on Management and Strategy: A Complexity Theory Approach." *Management Decision*, 45(1), 10–28.

McGuire, J.W. (1963). *Business and Society*. New York: McGraw Hill.

Mitleton-Kelly, E. (2003). *Complexity Systems and Evolutionary Perspectives on Organisations: The Application of Complexity Theory to Organisations*. Oxford: Elsevier, 1–31.

Mone, E., Eisinger, E., Guggenheim, K., Price, B., and Stine, C. (2011). "Performance Management at the Wheel: Driving Employee Engagement in Organizations." *Journal of Business Psychology*, 26(2), 205–212.

Morrison, K. (2010). "Complexity Theory, School Leadership and Management: Questions for Theory and Practice." *Educational Management Administration & Leadership*, 38(3), 374–393.

Morrison, M., Lumby, J., and Sood, K. (2006). "Diversity and Diversity Management: Messages from Recent Research." *Educational Management Administration & Leadership*, 34(3), 277–295.

Munchus, G. (1983). "Employer-Employee Based Quality Circles in Japan: Human Resource Policy Implications for American Firms." *Academy of Management Review*, 8(2), 255–261.

Nkomo, S. (2010). Unpacking Diversity, Grasping Inequality. Rethinking Difference through Critical Perspectives. *Organization*, 17(1), 9–29.

Noon, M (2007). "The Fatal Flaws of Diversity and the Business Case for Ethnic Minorities." *Work Employment Society*, 21(4), 773.

O'Toole, J (1995). *Leading Change: The Argument for Values-Based Leadership*. New York: Ballantine Books.

Rachele, J.S. (2013). "The Diversity Quality Cycle: Driving Culture Change through Innovative Governance." *AI & Society* (online copy available 2012).

Rapoport, R.N. (1970). "Three Dilemmas in Action Research: With Special Reference to the Tavistock Experience." *Human Relations*, 23(6), 499–513.

Roberson, L., Kulik, C., and Pepper, M.B. (2001). "Designing Effective Diversity Training: Influence of Group Composition and Trainee Experience." *Journal of Organizational Behavior*, 22(8), 871–885.

Sanchez, J.I. and Medkik, N. (2004). "The Effects of Diversity Awareness Training on Differential Treatment." *Group and Organization Management*, 29(4), 517–536.

Sanderson, I. (2001). "Performance Management, Evaluation and Learning in 'Modern' Local Government." *Public Administration*, 79(2), 297–313.

Schraad-Tischler, D. (2011). "Social Justice in the OECD: How Do Member States Compare?" Gütersloh: Bertelsmann Stiftung.

Schwartz, M.S. and Carroll, A.B. (2003). "Corporate Responsibility: A Three-Domain Approach." *Business Ethics Quarterly*, 13(4), 503–530.

Smith, L.T. (1999). *Decolonizing Methodologies: Research and Indigenous Peoples*. London: Zed Books.

Spicer, A., Alvesson, M. and Kärreman, D. (2009). "Critical Performativity: The Unfinished Business of Critical Management Studies." *Human Relations*, 62(4), 537–560.

Stewart, R.W. (2011). "You Support Diversity, But Are You Ethical? Examining the Interactive Effects of Diversity and Ethical Climate Perceptions on Turnover Intentions." *Journal of Business Ethics*, 100(4), 453–465.

Strike, V.M., Gao, T., and Bansal, P. (2006). "Being Good While Being Bad: Social Responsibility and the International Diversification of US Firms." *Journal of International Business Studies*, 37(6), 850–862.

Strother, J.B. (2002). "An Assessment on the Effectiveness of e-learning in Corporate Training Programs." *The International Review of Research in Open and Distance Learning*, 3(1), 1–17.

Susman, G.I. and Evered, R.D. (1978). "An Assessment of the Scientific Merits of Action Research." *Administrative Science Quarterly*, 23(4), 582–603.

Tatli, A. and Özbilgin, M.F. (2009). "Understanding Diversity Managers' Role in Organisational Change: Towards a Conceptual Framework." *Canadian Journal of Administrative Science*, 26(3), 244–258.

Walton, C. C. (1967). *Corporate Social Responsibilities*. Belmont: Wadsworth.

Wang, Y-S., Yang, H-Y., and Shee, D.Y. (2007). "Measuring e-learning Systems Success in an Organizational Context: Scale Development and Validation." *Computers in Human Behavior*, 23(4), 1792–1808.

Wood, D. (1991). "Corporate Social Performance Revisited." *Academy of Management Review*, 16(4), 691–718.

Zanoni, P. and Janssens, M. (2007). "Minority Employees Engaging with (Diversity) Management: An Analysis of Control, Agency, and Micro-Emancipation." *Journal of Management Studies*, 44(8), 1371–1397.

Zanoni, P. and Janssens, M. (2004). "Deconstructing Difference: The Rhetorics of HR Managers' Diversity Discourses." *Organization Studies*, 25, 55–74.

Zanoni, P., Janssens, M., Benschop, Y. and Nkomo, S. (2010). 'Unpacking Diversity, Grasping Inequality. Rethinking Difference through Critical Perspectives." *Organization*, 17(1), 9–29.

Index